Wheels of a Soul

For further information:

The Kabbalah Centre
155 E. 48th St., New York, NY 10017
1062 S. Robertson Blvd., Los Angeles, CA 90035

1.800.Kabbalah
www.kabbalah.com

Third Edition, January 2005
Printed in USA
ISBN 1-57189-301-6

Design: Hyun Min Lee

REINCARNATION
AND KABBALAH

Wheels

of

a Soul

K
KABBALAH
PUBLISHING

www.kabbalah.com™

RAV P. S. BERG

TABLE OF CONTENTS

ACKNOWLEDGMENTS

For my wife, Karen. In the vastness of cosmic space and the infinity of lifetimes, it is my bliss to be your soul mate and to share a lifetime with you.

INTRODUCTION

Many years have passed since I first met my master and teacher, Rav Yehuda Brandwein, and began the study of Kabbalah. I quickly realized that the topic of reincarnation is a central element of kabbalistic teachings. To my dismay, however, I also saw that very little information on this subject was available to the world. In fact, even individuals who had studied *The Zohar* and other kabbalistic texts—such as The Gates of Reincarnation, by Rav Isaac Luria—seemed unwilling to acknowledge the importance of reincarnation in these writings.

What's more, as I sought information on this topic through contact with other scholars, I was surprised at the bitter antagonism I encountered. It was as if the whole subject of reincarnation was best left alone.

To some extent, the attitude of these scholars toward a central topic of Kabbalah was not unlike their attitude toward Kabbalah as a whole. It was as if the whole subject was "too hot to handle." Now, however, it is time for all that to change with regard both to reincarnation and to Kabbalah in general. The wisdom of Kabbalah has been kept under wraps for centuries for want of an effective way to teach it. But today, when electricity, modern physics, and even relativity and quantum mechanics are familiar to the average person, Kabbalah can at last be made comprehensible to virtually everyone.

Kabbalah, which is as far removed from religion as are chemistry or physics, has always drawn hostile fire from religionists and scientists alike. Religionists feared the "blasphemy" of kabbalistic logic, and scientists feared the metaphysics that took Kabbalah beyond the scope of scientific thought. Not until the beginning of the 20th century, with the emergence of Einstein's theory of relativity, could the gap between scientist and kabbalist be bridged. Only now can the great kabbalistic doctrine of reincarnation—and even such universal principles as "love thy neighbor"—be explained with all the rigor of a mathematical formula.

As it undertakes such an explanation—with an eye toward a deeper understanding of the interplay of spiritual and scientific perspectives on the subject of reincarnation—this book will generate ideas that may initially seem esoteric and remote. I will therefore attempt to present them as clearly and concisely as possible.

Any serious discussion of reincarnation must begin with a definition of the term itself. For this, kabbalists go to the source of all wisdom, which is *The Bible*. There, Ecclesiastes 1:4 states, "One generation passes away and another generation comes, but the earth abides forever." As

The Zohar explains, what this verse really signifies is that the souls of the generation that have passed away will return as new incarnations in a future generation. The identities of the individual human beings will have changed, but at the soul level they will be the same. The issues that these souls need to deal with will also be the same, and they will remain so through many incarnations until those issues are finally resolved.

An identical thought is found in the Ten Commandments (Exodus 20:5), which state, "The sins of the fathers are remembered even unto the third and fourth generation." This passage does not mean, as some have erroneously contended, that God, in His wrath, will inflict punishment not only on the sinner but on the sinner's innocent grandchildren and great-grandchildren as well. Who could love and worship so vengeful a deity? *The Zohar* thus reveals the truth of this verse: The third and fourth generations are in fact identical to the first—one soul returning in the form of its own descendants so that it may correct the "sins of the fathers."

Insights on reincarnation abound in *The Bible*, and in this book we shall explore many of them. But the concept of reincarnation is by no means exclusive to Kabbalah. Reincarnation, for example, is the basis of most of the spiritual systems of India, whose hundreds of millions of followers accept the truth of reincarnation just as we accept the truth of gravity—as a natural and inevitable law that only a fool would question.

Beyond all doubt, reincarnation is one of the fundamental ideas of mankind—almost equal to belief in the exis-

tence of God Himself. Yet most authors writing on the subject show no knowledge of the origin of the idea. (*The Zohar*
clearly identifies that origin, and *The Gates of Reincarnation*
amplifies it.) Indeed, like every great and ancient idea, the
concept of reincarnation has come down to us shrouded in
superstition and misconception. "Reincarnation?" many people ask themselves. "Who wants to contemplate returning to
the world as a dog, or even an insect?" But even questions
such as these show that the topic of reincarnation has not
been understood at its most fundamental level. So let us
attempt to deal with that problem at the outset.

If a just God really exists, why is there so much misery
in the world? Why are there so many unearned gifts and
unpunished crimes? Why are innocent children stricken with
disease? Why are nursing mothers killed by drunken fools in
automobiles? Is it because God doesn't care? Or is He powerless to change these things? Moreover, if God created a
world as wretched as this one seems to be, what hope have we
to expect something better in Heaven?

One person may work hard all his life and at the very
end wind up an inpatient in a dreary hospital or charity
home. Another might inherit a vast estate and draw on the
luxuries of the world as if they were his personal fortune,
even though he may be an idler, a parasite, a useless burden
to society. Why should this be so? It would not be accurate
to say that it is a question of intellect, for many bright men
have failed where fools have not. Turn where we will, the
world is full of stark inequities and inexplicable contrasts.

Despite what the Declaration of Independence tells us,
all men are by no means created equal. Despite the orations

of politicians, we are unequal mentally, spiritually, and morally. Some among us have strong, healthy bodies, while others are frail and diseased. Some have quick minds; others are dull and limited.

The Bible tells us that behind every event there is God, but we cannot prove it is so by pointing to the condition of the world. To the contrary, chaos seems more amply in evidence than order. What is needed, therefore, is a master key with which to unlock this apparent chaos and find order within it. Reincarnation, stripped of superstition and half-truth, can provide just such a key. The purpose of this book is simply to present the vital truth of reincarnation.

When a child is born, we take for granted that its consciousness was created along with its body—that the internal aspect of the individual which we call a soul is present and will be there as long as the child continues to live. But why do we accept the proposition that this internal element determines our actions? Briefly stated, the reason is as follows: In a child, the development of consciousness occurs in parallel with the development of the body. And in old age, consciousness seems to deteriorate along with the physical self. Therefore, it would seem safe to assume that an internal process was at work that could not be seen directly but was present nonetheless.

The early development of children is so phenomenal in its scope that it cannot take place purely on a physical level. Such development is not simply referable to the bones, the muscles, and the brain when seen as purely material objects. Indeed, the human soul is no more dependent on the physical existence of the brain than a musician is dependent on the existence of his instrument—although both are necessary in order for music to be created. Only when we fully grasp this concept can we begin to approach the study of reincarnation. We must accept the first fundamental fact of reincarnation, which is that human consciousness—the soul—exists before birth.

And as regards the other end of life, in the course of this book I will attempt to make it quite clear that death comes only for the body. The soul lives eternally. Until we understand this, we are locked into a worldview that spans only 70 or 80 years and are prevented from embracing the universal consciousness that should really form the basis of our understanding.

My intention here is not to prove that reincarnation is a fact of nature, at least not in the sense of a conventionally experimental proof. Anyone who feels the need for strict scientific proof of reincarnation should recognize that as we probe deeper into the subatomic world or venture farther into the outer reaches of the universe, we inevitably find that experimental validation of any sort becomes increasingly difficult to accomplish.

In point of fact, the advance of scientific knowledge rarely forms a neat progression from theoretical prediction to observational proof. To the contrary, it is imagination—that sudden flash of insight—which has produced the greatest advances within the scientific community. The best science has always involved much more than the mere observation and organization of observable phenomena. Science is a way of discovering what our world is all about by advancing theories and then subjecting those theories to the test of observation and experiment. Yet between the abstract world of conjecture and the real world of experimentation, there will always exist a tension, and often even a conflict.

I have observed that the social and intellectual conditioning many people have received makes it impossible for them to survey the evidence supporting reincarnation with an unprejudiced eye. Just as it is daunting to convince a blind man that there are stars in the sky, so too may it seem difficult to break through the prejudices that the very thought of reincarnation provokes in many people. Yet if an operation could be performed to restore a blind man's sight, further debate would prove unnecessary. Accordingly, this book is offered as a kind of "surgical procedure" that will enable people to open the eye of inner vision and, in so doing, to understand that man is a creature who can achieve a truly exalted and eternal state of being.

Finally, I must emphasize that reincarnation is by no means a religious issue. It is not a question of faith or doctrine, but rather one of logic and reason. And while *The Bible* is a key source for understanding this issue, in these pages I will also present new material to demonstrate that reincarnation is very much a fact of life, regardless of the credo or doctrine under which that life is lived. This multifaceted approach will provide for all men and women one of the central reasons for their very existence. By explaining how we lived in the forgotten past, it will explain why we live as we do today. By explaining how we live today, it will empower us to take control of the future—and to claim the destiny of immortality that has always been intended for us.

1

RELIGION AND SCIENCE

M any people believe that the purpose of life is simply to survive. In their view, the goal of existence is simply to perpetuate itself; human beings live today in order that they—or their descendants—can live tomorrow. Others never give the matter much thought, preferring instead to enjoy the pleasures of the moment. Yet those who have been raised in kabbalistic or other spiritual traditions have their own beliefs concerning human life, including the existence of an immortal soul.

Regardless of their perspective on life's purpose or lack thereof, everyone is aware of the pain and suffering that exist in the world. Religion has attempted to provide an explanation for this. We have been told that our suffering is a test that has been given to us by God, with heaven or hell the reward or punishment that awaits us. Many people give credence to this explanation not because they have proof of its validity but because it has been handed down to them by their parents and prelates, who have picked it up from their parents and ravs and religious teachers—who have in turn ascribed it to the authority of *The Bible*.

Since the Renaissance, however, Western man has become increasingly skeptical of knowledge handed down on the strength of religious authority alone, be that authority a person or a book. Skepticism has been encouraged toward all doctrines that cannot be proven in a scientific laboratory.

Ptolemy, for example, said that the sun revolved around the earth. Later, however, Galileo developed an instrument that proved it was the other way around. Similarly, it was once almost universally believed that the earth was flat. But Magellan and other adventurers over-threw that assumption by sailing west and arriving back home from the east. By means of such demonstrations, man gradually came to see that the ancient authorities could indeed be proven wrong. Discovery after discovery shattered and disarranged the neat and orderly picture that mankind had believed to lie beyond challenge or dispute.

But what about spiritual matters? Will someone ever "discover" or "demonstrate" the existence of the human soul? And what of immortality? Who has come back to tell us about it? And heaven? Our telescopes show no evidence of it. God? God is the result, according to psychoanalysts, of a personality in need of a father figure.

Mechanistic science describes the universe as a colos-sal machine and man as a little machine—both made possible by an arrangement of atoms in a natural evolutionary process. In this way of thinking, suffering is simply man's inevitable struggle for survival and nothing more. Death is merely a dissolution of chemical elements. The "facts" are said to be in—just as they were when the sun was thought to revolve around a flat earth.

Science was born of our own five senses, and to a great extent it continues to rely on them. It has expanded our senses, to be sure, with microscopes, telescopes, and radar. It has systematized our observations through logical reasoning, mathematics, and experimental technologies. But science is still empirical, based on the testimony of our five senses.

For many thousands of years, questions about the essential nature of reality were resolved through references to faith and one of many varieties of divine beings. Then, with the rise of mechanistic science in the 17th and 18th centuries, a mechanical model of the universe began to replace the faith-based perspective. But while this model portrayed itself as something entirely new, it too was ultimately a form of faith. Consider the atom, for example. Whether the mechanical model could appropriately be applied to the atom was never questioned. This was not even experimentally investigated until the 20th century, when physicists were finally able to address matter's essence. With the most sophisticated technology the world had ever known, physicists were able to probe deeper and deeper into nature, uncovering one layer of matter after another. The existence of atoms was thus verified. Then the constituents of atoms were discovered—the nucleus, electrons, and finally protons, neutrons, and a host of subatomic particles. As the complex instruments of modern experimental physics penetrated into realms of nature far removed from our macroscopic environment, that world suddenly became accessible to our senses.

The subatomic world continues to lie beyond sensory perception, but with the help of modern instrumentation, investigators are now able to observe the properties of atoms and their constituents in an indirect way. Yet they can do so only through a chain of processes that culminates in the audible click of a Geiger counter or a dark spot on a photographic plate. What we thus see and hear are never the investigated phenomena themselves, but rather the consequences of those phenomena. Knowledge of matter at this level is no longer derived from direct sensory experience. Everyday language, therefore, which takes its images from the world of the senses, is no longer adequate to the task of describing observed phenomena. As we probe deeper and deeper into nature, we must abandon more and more of the images and concepts of ordinary language.

On this journey to the world of the infinitely small, the most important step from a philosophical standpoint was the first step. Once the physicist found himself dealing with the nonsensory experience of reality, he had to confront the paradoxical aspects of nature. When Einstein developed his theory of relativity, he destabilized physics by telling us that time is "elastic." Time, Einstein taught us, is not an absolute quantity, but is instead influenced by variables such as speed and mass. With this revolutionary insight, Einstein opened the door to the consideration of the validity of reincarnation.

Ironically, the very instruments we created with our five senses have now shown us that our sensory apparatus is itself imperfect—and hence inadequate to the task of revealing the world as it really is. Radio waves, radioactivity, and atomic energy are but a few of the phenomena that surround us but are utterly unavailable to unaided perception. The most minute particles of matter contain within them forces of a magnitude so great that our imaginations cannot encompass them—yet these particles are nowhere to be seen. In a similar manner, the phenomenon of human reproduction defies the imagination. Our five senses could never provide an understanding of how human conception is accomplished.

2

THE NEW AGE OF REALITY

W e are looking at the world through tiny peepholes. Our sensitivity to vibrations of light enables us to receive only a small fraction of the total light vibrations in existence. In the same way a 50 cent dog whistle will summon your pet, but you will not hear it because its frequency exceeds the uppermost limit of your sensitivity.

There are many animals and insects whose range of seeing, hearing, or smell is different from our own. Consequently, their universe contains much that we cannot perceive. This is a curious spectacle indeed: proud man, exceeded in his sensory capacity by dogs, birds, and even fish. In light of this, thinking people are forced to question their perception of reality, and to long for insight into some of these great invisibilities.

But suppose we were trained to use our sensory equipment in such a way that our sensitivity to light and sound

were slightly enhanced. Would we not become aware of
many objects that were previously undetectable to us? Or
suppose a few of us were born with an expanded range of
perception. Would not those few among us see and hear
things the rest of us did not? History provides a number of
instances of just such enhanced sensitivity—and yet the people who possessed them were not always treated kindly.
Rav Shimon bar Yohai had awesome wisdom and power at
his fingertips. Yet he and his son were forced to hide in a cave
for years in order to reveal *The Zohar*.

When nature fails to provide it, science has also shown
itself capable of expanding man's quest for knowledge, often
into areas that have been overlooked or ignored by main-
stream scientists. Semyon and Valentina Kirlian offer an
excellent example of this. In 1958, these Russian scientists,
using a photographic technique that had been known since
the 1890s, captured on film for the first time an impression
of the biological field that constitutes the human aura. This
process, called electrophotography, also made it possible to
examine the pattern of luminescence around dozens of mate-
rials—including rubber, coins, leaves, paper, and textiles.

The Kirlians found that the structural details of ema-
nations were different for each item they tested and pho-
tographed. The most significant result of their study, however, was the discovery that living things have patterns that are
totally different from those emanated by inanimate objects.
Whereas a metal coin is surrounded by a constant, unvarying
aura, a living being produces a picture of myriad sparkling,
shooting, flashing lights that glow like jewels.

In reporting the results of their breakthrough, the Russian scientists wrote:

> What we saw in the panorama through the microscope and our optical instruments seemed like the control board of a huge computer. Here and there, lights brightened and dimmed, signaling internal processes. If something went wrong inside, or if conditions needed adjustment, the engineer at the control box could read the signals in the lights.

In living things, we see the signals of the inner state of the organism reflected in the brightness, dimness, or color of the flares. The inner life of the activities of a human being is written in these light hieroglyphs. We have created an apparatus with which to write these hieroglyphs, but to read them, we're going to need help.

A book entitled *Behind the Iron Curtain* offered additional information about the Kirlians:

> The Kirlian team was working that evening on the photographs when something strange happened. From testing leaves from various plants, they knew that each species had its own unique energy pattern, like individual television set patterns broadcasting from each type of plant. But the photos of the twin leaves that the scientists had given them differed sharply from each other. Were the leaves from two dif-

ferent species of plants? Had they made an error? They did picture after picture with the same results.

The Kirlians could, in other words, confirm only the individuality of each entity tested, however closely related that entity might have been to its twin. Suddenly, in a world in which paranormal, metaphysical phenomena were seen to exist, and in which the aura of an individual entity could prove to be different even from its twin, our five senses had become thoroughly inadequate guides.

3

THE DILEMMA OF
UNEXPECTED EVENTS

In light of the amazing revelations of contemporary science, we can no longer rely on simplistic explanations to account for the events of our daily lives, no matter how convenient those explanations might seem. We can no longer dismiss unexplained happenings as mere coincidence.

Few knew this better than Dr. J. B. Rhine of Duke University. Beginning in 1930, this visionary scientist and his associates studied the telepathic and clairvoyant faculties of man. After conducting closely controlled experiments using scientific methods, Rhine discovered that many people exhibit evidence of extrasensory perception under laboratory conditions. Meticulous statistical techniques have since been used to assess Dr. Rhine's experiments, and mathematically speaking, they have indicated that the results he achieved could not possibly be attributed to chance.

There is a growing body of evidence that telepathic and clairvoyant powers exist in the human mental apparatus. The potential usefulness of these powers has not even been scratched, and that potential is enormous. Clearly if a man possesses a means of cognition that does not depend on his five senses—if he can, under certain conditions, see what is taking place elsewhere with his mind rather than with his eyes—then man possesses a supremely powerful tool with which to obtain knowledge about himself and the universe. It's high time man started to use it!

We have achieved great things through the centuries, but for all our strength and versatility, humanity remains fragile and vulnerable. For all our accomplishments in the realms of art, science, and culture, we are still perplexed by our suffering and that of our loved ones, from birth until death. Of late, however, we have penetrated the inner recesses of the atom, and now—with emerging discoveries about extrasensory perception and the relationship between the conscious and subconscious mind—we are on the brink of penetrating the inner recesses of our own being. Now, at long last, we can find satisfying answers to the most fundamental riddles of our existence. Now we will be able to understand the reasons for our birth and learn where it really leads, other than death.

4

Reincarnation and Human Suffering

"If God is good, loving, merciful, and just, why do many millions of innocent people suffer while the guilty prosper and go free?"

That question is almost as old as humankind itself, and the answer to it is just as old. Yet it can be understood only through metaphor.

The Hebrew word for reincarnation is *Gilgul Neshamot*—which means, literally, "wheel of the soul." We must look toward this vast metaphorical wheel, with souls studding its rim like stars on the edge of a galaxy, if we are to see beyond the appearance of innocence punished and evil rewarded. *Gilgul Neshamot* is a wheel that is constantly turning. And with its motion, souls come and go in a cycle of birth, death, and rebirth.

The same process occurs within an individual body in the course of a single lifetime. Birth, growth, reproduction, and death—new life is produced by old, giving rise to continuity of physical form.

Understanding this process at the physical level is the key to a truthful view of life's continuum. Yet most who really consider it will be surprised at how much is taken for truth without any real thought at all.

The whole direction of physical evolution is from the simple to the complex. At one end of the organic series is the single cell. At the other is the extraordinarily complex human body, with its countless cells organized into organs, bones, and vast networks of nerves and brain tissue. Our bodies are constantly enacting this progression. The brain of a baby has little capacity for conscious awareness, but as children grow, their minds becomes more formidable—not so much because of growth in height or weight but by virtue of a steady strengthening of consciousness. Eventually, in old age, the power of consciousness again recedes—until at death the instrument of consciousness, the brain, is destroyed. But this destruction does not extend to the soul or even to consciousness itself. Only the instrument has ceased to exist. The process of evolution continues, and understanding this is essential to understanding the concept of reincarnation.

Throughout nature, mineral forms are broken apart to furnish food for plants. Plants are in turn sacrificed for animals, and animals are sacrificed for man. From a physical perspective, nature is little more than a slaughterhouse. Consequently, since nature patently cares so little for physical bodies, it is easy to wonder if anything has a purpose.

Still, something in our universe keeps the continuum going. Growth, like the wheel, has no beginning and no end.

But to view life merely as a beginning and an end is akin to viewing a tree in a forest and saying there is only the tree. Caught up in the continuum of time and motion, we can easily lose our bearings. Everything in life, without exception, operates as a wheel. Yet most people find it impossible to look beyond the present moment. It is impossible to see that in coming to earth many times, we gather experience and pass from one grade to another, just as we did as children growing up.

In the past, primitive societies evolved from a root civilization to what might be called a moral civilization. What we have reaped, for good or evil, is a continuous progression of experiences that can be seen as incarnation following incarnation. We grow continually from agrarian societies to cities, from war to peace and to war again, never really seeing beyond our place on the rim of the wheel. We blindly accept the motion of the wheel that constitutes our lives without ever questioning to what end it turns. But a new age has dawned, and all that is about to change.

Now that we are living in the Age of Aquarius, the teachings of Kabbalah are available to all who have a desire to learn. Because of the ever-increasing volume of Light that has come down to us from the sages of the past, we are moving from darkness to a new awareness of an ongoing movement in eternity. We are now capable, if we so choose, of grasping the concept of the soul's participation in the turning of the wheel, unlimited by identification with a particular physical body.

Because the Age of Aquarius is truly the Age of Enlightenment, it may now be possible for even the most skeptical among us to understand that knowledge acquired in past lives remains with us today. We might even dare to say that people who learned such things in the past have returned to this life with knowledge and experience to share with the present era.

Let us now return to the frustrating inequity of human suffering. By far the most common sources of such suffering are disease and old age. For all our scientific advances, we have not even scratched the surface in our struggle against these two adversaries. Nor have we shown any progress in solving the riddle of death itself. Fire, flood, disease, and disaster are only the outer threats to peace, happiness, and life. Inwardly the battle rages on against selfishness, stupidity, frivolity, hypocrisy, and greed—all endless sources of pain. Moments of despair are interspersed with flights of fancy, high elation. and the enduring hope that at the center of it all there is a haven of love, beauty, and understanding. Still the wheel turns, leaving us to struggle in a mire of confusion, forever wondering about our purpose. "Who am I? Why am I here? Where am I going?"

Until these most basic questions of existence have been answered, nothing can be answered. Until the reasons for pain have been elucidated, nothing can be explained. Until the suffering of the most insignificant creature has been accounted for, nothing has been accounted for, and our philosophical grasp of life remains woefully incomplete.

5

REINCARNATION AND
THE BIBLE

We are taught from childhood that God rewards our good deeds and punishes our transgressions. It is as if God were standing somewhere above us in the manner of a stern parent, saying, "Oh, you're good? Here's a piece of candy"—or "Oh, you're bad? You'll get a spanking." Never believe this! Such a simplistic view gives no credit to The Creator and even less to His creation.

Most of us, be we Jew or Christian, have been raised with the concept of an immortal soul that resides somewhere in the interior of our being. We have been taught that suffering is essentially a test that is given to us by God. Heaven or hell will be the reward or the punishment that awaits us when life is over.

Kabbalah teaches instead that reward and punishment are no different from the electrical socket in your living room. Plug light into it and the room will be illuminated.

Stick your finger into it and you will receive a nasty shock. The results are neither reward nor punishment, but merely the consequence of individual action and the exercise of free will.

Still, millions continue to cling to the scenario of reward and punishment—not because they have proof of its validity, but because they think *"The Bible* tells me so." And for much the same reason, millions refuse even to contemplate the possibility of reincarnation. "Where," they might ask, "is reincarnation mentioned in *The Bible*, whose authority we all so highly esteem?"

Actually, the Book of Exodus offers a full explanation not just of reincarnation, but also of the effect of reincarnation in terms of parents and children, brothers and sisters, and how all interrelate in the immediate environment. These insights, however, rest on our ability to remember our past lives. Indeed, one of the strongest arguments against reincarnation lies in the question "If we were born before, why don't we remember? And even if we did live before, why are we being punished now for things we can't even remember having done in some existence long ago?"

In Exodus 16, The Creator forbids the making of pagan gods and commands, "Thou shalt not bow down unto them nor serve them. For I, the Lord thy God, am a jealous God, visiting the iniquities of the fathers upon the children unto the third and fourth generation of them that hate me." This particular verse has been the subject of extensive debate and much criticism. The controversy, of course, centers on the injustice of punishing succeeding generations for the sins of one man or woman.

The laws of heredity, which are only now beginning to be understood, might at first glance seem to support a literal view of this biblical passage—of parental sin being passed along to offspring. Short-term greed, for example, has in fact engendered pollution of our air and water supplies, and those sins have indeed been passed along to our children, often several generations down the line, in the form of birth defects and congenital disorders. There is, however, one apparent paradox in human development that heredity fails to explain. In the lower animal kingdom, one encounters little difficulty in formulating a system of hereditary law. Kittens are virtual carbon copies of cats. Baby birds need no flying lessons once their feathers have developed. Man alone is different. The often vast divergence in mental and moral values between parents and their children seems to go well beyond the boundaries set by any genetic blueprint.

The verse in Exodus regarding "sins of the father" does not mean what it seems to mean. To the contrary, it holds much deeper significance. What it really signifies is that a given individual, when sent into this world for the purpose of correction, must complete that correction or else return. The Bible never meant to imply that an innocent one would pay for sins committed by his father, but rather that the individual who has committed those sins literally is the father, having returned in the third or fourth generation to resume the task of correction where he left off. In a literal sense of the word, the individual becomes his own great- or great-great-grandchild.

The great Kabbalist Rav Isaac Luria taught that the number of times this cycle must be repeated depends on the individual soul. If that soul lives one lifetime with no progress, it is allowed to return three more times at a maximum, at which point total failure will result in that soul's reversion to the abyss.

In a literal translation of Exodus, the word generation is not mentioned. And with that deletion, the meaning of this passage becomes clear. A man or woman may return three more times, for a total of four lives. If progress is made in any of these incarnations, no further limit is imposed on the number of reincarnations needed to complete the mission of correction. Even if progress is made, however, the danger of plunging backward is always present.

6

REINCARNATION AT
LOWER LEVELS

K abbalah teaches us that if the weight of *tikune* (correction) is sufficiently heavy, a human soul may find itself reincarnated into the body of an animal, a plant, or even a stone. As incredible as that statement may seem, it will elucidate many mysteries that have confounded man from his earliest beginnings to the present time. It will also explain much that psychiatrists have vainly attempted to describe as "mental illness."

For the soul of a murderer, reincarnation into a human body is not likely to result in anything beyond more murder, since the act of taking lives is the utmost manifestation of the individual's desire to receive. From a kabbalistic standpoint, therefore, it is possible that such a soul will return to the physical plane as an inanimate object, in which the desire to receive is at a bare minimum. In such a hell of total confinement, a soul would be able to shed the evil husks of negative

energy, called *klipot*, that have covered it. It would then be
free of the awful temptation to kill.

Not all who fall under the weight of their crimes,
however, find themselves imprisoned in stone. Depending on
the gravity of the *klipot* that their negative energy has
manufactured, they may also return as animals or plants, and
in so doing will leave vivid traces of what folklore calls
"hauntings."

In the winter months especially, when days are short
and darkness is the rule, we often hear tales of sounds ema-
nating from seemingly inanimate objects, or of stark and
leafless trees that seem to brood with malevolent intelligence. Take these anecdotes as fairy tales or as legitimate
metaphysical phenomena, but do not dismiss what in
Hebrew is known as *ubar*—a soul that attaches itself to the
unwary when the very animal or vegetable matter into which
they have been incarnated are consumed.

Recent history abounds with stories of perfectly
rational, even kind people who for no apparent reason have
suddenly turned into implacable and merciless killers. I know
a woman who has twice been admitted to a psychiatric ward
because she felt she was being bombarded by evil spirits. I
can testify that this woman is as normal as anyone who has
been pronounced mentally fit—but that definition is itself
suspect. I believe that between 70 and 80% of all human
beings display "abnormal behavior" at one time or another,
and in most cases an invading spirit of evil is the root cause.
Indeed, rites of exorcism might heal far more of the so-called
mentally ill than all the tools of the psychiatric community
combined, be they drugs or electroshock therapy.

To illustrate this point, a tale is told of Shmuel Vital, the son of the great Kabbalist Chaim Vital. Shmuel Vital was in Egypt when he was summoned to a young woman who had been stricken mute and paralyzed two months after her marriage had taken place. Given the sudden onset of her affliction, Vital suspected that an evil spirit had managed to invade the woman's being.

Suddenly a male voice emanated from the stricken woman—the soul of a man who had loved the woman and had been consumed with jealousy when she had married another. For this reason, the man told Vital, he had possessed the woman and had rendered her incapable of functioning as a wife to his rival. An exorcist was thus summoned who was able to draw out the possessing spirit and enclose it in a bottle, which was then buried in the sand. Had the unfortunate girl lived today, the fate that awaited her would probably have been a lifetime of confinement in a psychiatric ward.

Further biblical support for reincarnation can be found in the verse from Exodus that reads, "Now these are the ordinances which thou shalt set before them . . . should man acquire a Hebrew slave." What follows might at first seem little more than a list of rules governing the ownership and treatment of slaves—ordinances that are now irrelevant in that the institution of slavery, at least in its formal sense, has been abolished in virtually every nation on earth. But the term *slave*, in the case of the verse cited above, is only a figure of speech referring to a vessel that contains—and thus reveals—the means by which souls return into this world. This slavery is nothing other than that of every human being to the energy of the physical body.

Another entire book would be needed to detail the specifics of the Exodus passage, but these are covered extensively in *The Zohar*. Briefly, the passage tells us that souls will be judged according to the sin that has been committed in a prior lifetime, and incarnations will continue until all of those sins have been corrected.

7

The Math Connection

A common objection to the concept of reincarnation is mathematical in nature. If the number of souls is finite and souls keep returning through reincarnation, how can there be an increase in population.

Kabbalah teaches, however, that Adam himself was the repository of all the souls that would ever exist on earth. His own soul was thus infinitely divisible. When Adam sinned in Eden, his Vessel was shattered, and his corporeal soul was fragmented into what the kabbalists calls "sparks"—each spark as unique as the double helix of DNA that determines the characteristics of each individual. In this way, the earth was sown with souls, while millions more lay in metaphysical silos waiting to begin the cycle of birth, life, death, and rebirth. The concept of souls as sparks also explains the psychological variations found among different human beings. With progress in modern science, we have become acutely aware that the human organism is not just a physical structure made up of cells and molecules. At the most fundamental level, we are pure energy, and this energy is animated by an intelligence that is constantly at work in our bodies.

When the soul of Adam became fragmented, the endless volume of intelligence became incarnated in a vast number of bodies, each with its own identity. Intelligences that were once part of Adam's brain incarnated as brilliant people whose work related to intellectual activity. Intelligences that were part of Adam's fingers were incarnated as human beings whose activities involved working with the hands. Each and every force of energy- intelligence from the first human being migrated with its particular DNA formula, thus accounting for the countless variations found among people on earth.

8

THE BODY AND
INTERNAL FUNCTION

A ny discussion of reincarnation must of necessity include a discussion of consciousness and its origin. But Kabbalah's view of consciousness can be made clear only if we discard the notion that consciousness is dependent on the physical brain. If this were the case, consciousness would die when the body dies. Each individual, however, is composed of two parts: the physical, external self and the spiritual, inner self. The body may lapse into coma, but the inner self can remain totally aware of what is happening—a point that is supported by recent studies of near-death experiences.

Many studies of near-death experiences make reference to a tunnel with a bright light at its end. This phenomenon is also described in *The Zohar*: Upon the death of the physical body, the soul travels to Hebron, where Adam resides, making the journey by means of a long tunnel. In fact, this post-death tunnel is described in many spiritual traditions and can hardly be the product of a particular culture or religion. How can this common thread be possible? The kabbalists explain that consciousness is immortal. Certain memories extend "back to the future," crossing the threshold that separates life and death. Thus, although our memories of the other dimension are not ordinarily accessible, they are always present, like bits of memory in a computer's hard drive. And like any other form of energy, these memories can never be destroyed. They are stored and remain viable through each of our many incarnations.

9

POWER OF THE MIND

Consider this miracle: A man and a woman, through sexual intercourse, create another human being who comes into existence with all of his or her faculties and potentials in place from the very moment of birth. Without disputing the presence of God, why is the exercise of His power dependent on the sexual passion of man? And if a child's moral, spiritual, and mental abilities are present at birth, why are they so different in each individual? They range from the amorality and ignorance of the savage to the wisdom and ethical stature of the saint, and the differences in their destinies are vast.

Only the preexistence of the soul and an understanding of reincarnation can account for these differences. In essence, the entire physical process of conception and birth is designed to supply the soul with a physical body that will conform to the behavior of that soul as it existed in a prior lifetime.

Reincarnation also sheds light on the subject of children who are born deformed, or who die when they are still
very young. These are issues that have tormented parents by
the millions in every succeeding generation.

What is the meaning and purpose of such a situation?
For the answer to that question in the case of every birth that
has ever taken place or that ever will occur, Kabbalah directs
us to one specific condition at one specific moment in time:
the thoughts of the parents during sexual intercourse.

With physical energy provided by the mother, whose
metaphysical structure is negative, and soul energy chan-
neled through the positive aspect of the father, the power of
the parents' thoughts at the moment of ejaculation will
determine the characteristics of the child's body and spirit.
But these thoughts do even more. They select the very soul
that will occupy the body of their offspring by setting up the
environmental conditions necessary for any given soul to
complete its correction, or tikune.

A soul with a dark and heavy tikune, subject to live
under grim circumstances that afford a chance of karmic
redemption, will home in swiftly on conceptive thoughts of
anger, frustration, and destruction. If the thoughts of the
future parents are dominated by lust and motivated solely by
the desire for self-indulgence, their child will reflect selfishness and lust, just as the child conceived in a moment of deep
love and mutual understanding will reflect those positive
characteristics. Every soul returning to the world must find a
place in which conditions will be similar to those left behind
in the prior lifetime. In this way, parents and children are

brought together as if they had selected one another from a cosmic catalog.

There are, to be sure, a few exceptions to this rule. Some rare souls whose tikunes have been completed return to this plane with a mission for mankind that has nothing to do with personal karma. Rav Shimon bar Yohai had no karmic reason to walk this earth again 2000 years ago, but he returned because he alone could reveal the wisdom of *The Zohar*. In a similar manner, RavIsaac Luria appeared solely to interpret *The Zohar* and to spread its wisdom.

10

SOULMATES

For the vast majority of couples, bringing a child into the world means opening a channel for a soul that may enhance their lives or make them miserable. This determination is made on the basis of their attitudes at the moment of that channel's creation. For those who know nothing of Kabbalah or who have no understanding of reincarnation, this is a frightening prospect, implying as it does that couples gamble with their very lives in the act of procreation.

However, happy are those who may be soulmates at such a moment. Soulmates are truly one being. They are so joyful in each other's company that no unloving thought could intrude on the act of making love.

Before the sin of Adam created darkness and brought about the world in which we live, all male and female souls were one. But *The Zohar* tells us that The Creator split each of these souls, creating male and female above before Adam and Eve were made manifest below. Soulmates are those two halves of a single soul that are brought back together again, usually after they have wandered through many lifetimes searching for one another and fulfilling their tikune.

As a general rule, soulmates may meet and marry only after their karmic debt has been paid. For this reason, few couples in the world at any given time are true soulmates. Moreover, of the two sexes, men find it more difficult to complete their tikune. They are, perhaps, more willful and stubborn than women, who often accomplish soul correction in as little as a single lifetime on this earth. Indeed, when a woman whose karmic debt is balanced returns to this world, it is usually for the purpose of aiding a man who is struggling to balance his own debt. This aid, however, is not always gentle. A man who has repeatedly failed to achieve soul correction may be given a woman who will make his life anything but pleasant. Divorce and remarriage may occur, often several times, yet none of those unions will have been wasted. Every one of them was meant to be, for the sake of whatever lesson a man is intended to learn.

11

REINCARNATION AND EVIL

E ach of our incarnations is but a continuation of the preceding one. Thus, even a short life serves a purpose—whether it is a lesson the soul of a child needs to learn, or a lesson needed by the soul of a grieving parent. However tragic the circumstances may be, nothing is ever lost or forgotten. No matter how short or tragic a life may be, it either adds something of value to the memory of the soul or allows for the payment of a debt.

In this way, an understanding of reincarnation illuminates the problem of evil. We have been taught that God is good, loving, just, and all-powerful. Yet who among us has not wondered why His world is filled with such misery and injustice? Religious leaders and philosophers alike have thrown up their hands at this dilemma, but few have seen that the answer lies in reincarnation.

The degree of evil and injustice on earth has nothing whatsoever to do with God. War, murder, violence, deceit,

and oppression are not the result of His will. Rather, they are
the result of millions of souls struggling to balance their
karmic debt and failing. Now, in the Age of Aquarius, with
time winding down to the coming of the Messiah and a pass-
ing away of the old order, souls laden with evil are flocking
to the material plane in desperate need of correction. For
this reason, it is hardly surprising that evil moves in high
profile and that acts of evil now seem worse than they have
ever been before.

Science, of course, continues to insist that crime is
born solely of social and economic conditions and that
human characteristics are exclusively a product of heredity.
Yet while a child may look exactly like his or her parents, vast
differences in moral fiber and attitude are frequently in evidence. These differences cannot be explained by heredity
alone; nor can the fact that parents may exercise great influence over one child and none whatsoever over another. Such
differences are not due to divine favoritism or to the blind
workings of the laws of heredity. Rather, they are based on
the differences between one soul and another. Yet these differences are never indiscriminately bestowed on us. To the
contrary, we ourselves bring our own characteristics into
being. We are self-evolved. And this must be so if we are to
gain the merit of our actions. Evil is present in order for us
to make a choice between good and evil. If only good existed, we would be robots, not human beings.

12

The Man Who Returned
As His Nephew

No discipline stands to benefit more from the secrets of human reincarnation than do the behavioral sciences. Practitioners of these disciplines continue to be baffled by the fact that hospital wards remain filled with the so-called mentally ill, notwithstanding the many advances that have been made in recent decades. In these circles, reincarnation is still considered unworthy of scientific inquiry. Yet case histories can be found that illustrate its truth beyond mere argumentation or theory.

One such case began on a beautiful summer day, when I received a frantic telephone call at our apartment in Ramat Gan, in Israel.

"Our family must have an immediate appointment with you," cried Mrs. R.B., a student at The Kabbalah Centre in Beer Sheba. "The accidental death or the possible murder of my brother never ceases to haunt us, and my mother has become increasingly morbid and depressed. She demands to know, once and for all, whether her son committed suicide, was intentionally murdered by his best friend, or was accidentally shot by him."

The son had been found dead 11 months before. After an exhaustive investigation, the police had closed his file without reaching any conclusion as to the circumstances of his death.

I arranged a meeting at which all members of the immediate family were to be present. I felt this would be the only way I could obtain the kind of information I sought—information that, while appearing to be of little or no consequence, often produces the missing parts of the human jigsaw puzzle. From the outset, I also made it clear that our investigation would ultimately lead to a direct confrontation with 300 years of speculation regarding man's nature.

The ancient kabbalists tell us that human beings consist of a mystical compound of physical matter and intangible spirit. Despite resistance from their peers, prominent scientists from fields as diverse as neurobiology and quantum physics have recently begun to concur, admitting to the possible existence of such distinctly unscientific entities as the immortal human soul and a spiritually structured universe. Drawing from *The Zohar* and from Rav Isaac Luria's *Gates of Reincarnation*, I have come to the conclusion that the individuality of human beings is not a result of a unique genetic code, but rather that personal DNA structure is a product of the metaphysical, individual immortal soul that becomes manifest through the physical individual. Much the same relationship exists between the seed and the tree. The entire potential state of the tree clearly exists in the seed long before it becomes manifest in the form of leaves and branches.

Operating from this proposition, we embarked on our effort to address the young man's tragic and untimely death. From the outset, I was aware that most of the information I sought in this fact-finding mission would appear to be of little significance to our case. I was certain, however, that the immortal, nonmaterial intelligence of the soul was capable of influencing matter, and that this connection would yield vital information congruent with the principles of the *tikune* concept of reincarnation.

The facts were these: Late one day in the previous summer, Aryeh, a soldier in the Israeli army and a resident of Beer Sheba, had left his home with his closest friend to enjoy a day off and find some relief from the summer heat. By 3:30 P.M., Aryeh was dead.

Aryeh's friend was found on the road in a state of shock and confusion, with no memory whatsoever of the events that had just taken place. All he could say was that Aryeh lay dead of a gunshot wound. A six-month police investigation followed but shed no further light on the matter. Had Aryeh taken his own life? Had his friend accidentally shot him? Had he been murdered? The police could not say.

To learn the truth, I first ascertained the victim's correct biblical name and his date of birth, based on the Hebrew lunar calendar.

I learned that Aryeh had been born on the ninth day of the Hebrew month of Heshvan, which in that year corresponded to the civil date of November 12. In Hebrew, Aryeh means lion, and he had met his death in the cosmic month of Leo.

Armed with this knowledge, I continued to ask Aryeh's family one seemingly insignificant question after another in the hopes of finding the particular thought or event on which our mystery might turn. That pivotal moment came when the brother of the deceased mentioned his own son, whom he had named after the slain young man.

"What is your son's date of birth?" I asked.

"The 29th day in the Hebrew month of Nissan," the brother replied.

I could scarcely restrain myself, because that was the clue I had been looking for!

At that moment, I recalled an important principle of the *tikune* process of reincarnation. In his writings, the Ari discusses the consequences of accidental murder in light of the soul's knowledge of past incarnations and the *tikune* requirements of those lifetimes. Just as physical DNA determines the color of an individual's eyes, so too can metaphysical DNA ascertain the reason a murder has been committed.

"What—and for what purpose—predetermines, directs, and has brought into existence the circumstances surrounding a nonpremeditated murder or accidental homicide?" asks the Ari. On the basis of a verse in Exodus, the Ari concludes that accidental death may already have been predetermined and the circumstances that surround it already known. The Bible states, "[If a man slay another] and the slayer lie not in wait but God cause it to come to hand, then I will appoint thee a place whither he may flee."

The Ari further notes that the passage cited above contains an apparent contradiction. If the fatal blow to which it refers was indeed an accident, then what is meant by "but

God cause it to come to hand"? This passage implies that the slaying was predetermined by a prior intelligence.

Grappling with the metaphysical genetic code as a scientist would with the forces that direct the behavior of physical living systems, the Ari refers to a victim who was already a condemned man before his slaying. The Ari further states that the accidental death was an opportunity to provide the victim with the earliest possible reincarnation.

"Furthermore," says the Ari, "through the methodology of kabbalistic letters, the appropriate time for non-premeditated murder victims to return for *tikune* purposes is during the Hebrew month of Elul *[Virgo]*."

Aryeh had not yet reached his 20th birthday, so he could not have met his death as a result of wrongdoing on his part. According to Talmudic interpretation, anyone under the age of 20 cannot be condemned to death for premeditated murder. Therefore, the young man's death could only have been the product of a principle in the *tikune* process of reincarnation.

I then proceeded to calculate the time of conception of the child born to Aryeh's brother following his death. To my surprise, I found that conception had to have occurred in the month of Elul *[Virgo]*. The brother's child had been born on the civil date of April 26, or the Hebrew date of the 29th of Nissan *[Aries]*, placing the date of conception in the month of Elul. This, in addition to the fact that the child had been named Aryeh, confirmed for me that the two Aryehs were one and the same, with the elder having been reincarnated in the form of his own brother's son.

This conclusion, along with the circumstances surrounding it, answered the grieving family's question. Their
son had not committed suicide and had not been the victim
of a premeditated slaying. The proof of this point lay in the
conception of a new, yet old, Aryeh in the Hebrew month of
Elul, along with the naming of the child after the victim.
This was a powerful example of the *tikune* process at work.

When I explained my findings to the young man's family, the effect was profound. The spirit of the deceased and
newly born Aryeh produced a moral awareness of sufficient
intensity to alter their lives and make them infinitely more
loving toward one another. Once people become aware of
the spiritual energies that have previously been invisible to
them, their whole concept of reality changes at the most
basic level. The world of their five senses is no longer
enough. What previously seemed to be "everything" is now
understood to represent only the tiniest glimpse of what
"everything" really represents.

13

RECALLING PAST LIVES

Reincarnation is intrinsic to each of us, so it is incumbent on us all to use its precepts to enhance our lives. There are many ways in which we can achieve this objective, and memory is one of them. In fact, the recollection of past lives constitutes an overwhelming proof of reincarnation. At the same time, however, it is also the most difficult proof to achieve, since few of us can summon such memories at will. Of course, the fact that we cannot remember a prior existence is no more proof that a past life did not exist than not remembering what we had for breakfast last week constitutes proof that we did not eat. Most of us cannot remember the first four years of our lives, even though those years are the most important ones in terms of our physical and emotional development.

According to *The Zohar*, we never forget anything. Just as satellites monitor and record almost everything that moves on earth, so too does human consciousness act as an all-seeing camera—one that records everything that takes place in an individual's lifetime. The problem, however, as computer technicians would say, lies in "accessing the data." Efforts to achieve this access have taken two forms in recent decades. Hypnotism is one such form, but it is a method that does not work.

Once an individual has entered a hypnotic trance and is no longer bound by the laws of the physical world, he should, at least in theory, gain access to a dimension of time that is not governed by this plane of existence. In point of fact, a hypnotized person may indeed feel disassociation from his body—but at the same time, he is still responding to the questions and suggestions of the inquirer. Only when there is a complete disconnect with the physical body can knowledge of past incarnations be realized.

One technique that does work is meditation. To be sure, there are enough forms and variations of kabbalistic meditation to fill a book of its own. Without going into specifics, however, a general profile of the practice can be offered here.

A good way to begin any meditation is to spend a few minutes silently asking, "What do I want?" Since most of us would be quick to say, "I know what I want," this question is seldom posed. But asking it with an open mind can open the door to a higher cosmic consciousness.

Most of us go through life allowing our bodies to re--exively handle life's every function. But there is a soul within each of us, and with very little effort that soul can travel to other dimensions. It is much like a man out walking his dog: If the dog is not brought to heel, he will walk ahead and appear to be leading but will constantly stop and look back to make sure his master is following. The same principle applies to the body and the soul—and with just a little determination, the soul can leave the body to journey back in time.

As we have seen, when the soul leaves the body it travels through a long tunnel. According to *The Zohar*, that tunnel leads to Hebron in Israel and to the cave of Machpelah, where Abraham, Isaac, Jacob, and even Adam and Eve lie buried. Regarding these great souls, one point must always be emphasized: These are the patriarchs of all humanity, not just those of the Jewish and Christian religions, for whom *The Bible* is the principal spiritual text.

One does not have to be physically dead in order for the soul to make this journey. Any out-of-body experience gained through meditation will take the soul over the same route. To move back in time and into other incarnations, all the meditator need do is envision the tunnel, ensuring only that he stops as soon as he sees light at the end. To go all the way and leave the tunnel where the light marks its boundary is to leave the body through death, and thus there is a measure of danger in this meditation. Some have reportedly been unable to return, but I myself have known only one person who experienced difficulty in doing so. So this method, if prudently handled, is among the best.

Even without meditation, however, our lives abound with clues to what has come before. One of the most telling clues is the experience of fear.

Almost all of us have been plagued by one or more irrational, unfounded fears. Heights give some of us vertigo;

tight spaces afflict others with claustrophobia; and the mere sight of a cat causes still others to tremble with fright. Indeed, phobias such as these can become so all-consuming that they coalesce into one great "global phobia," whose effect is such that its victims cannot even leave their homes.

"Unfounded" is an excellent adjective here because it signifies that we have not yet "found" the reason underlying such fears. In fact, the fears aroused by phobias offer an excellent indicator of events that have taken place in a prior incarnation. For this reason, phobias should not be treated with drugs or therapy until they have first been closely examined for the valuable information and clues they contain.

Just as any meditation should begin with the question "What do I want?" a meditation to overcome phobia should begin with the question "Why do I really have this fear?"

Just asking the question plants the seed of the answer. But what is hidden is not the information itself. What is hidden is the desire to request the information. Dig it out and you will begin to make progress toward alleviating the fear through the memory of what caused it.

14

BREAKING THE CODE

The *Zohar* states, "It is now fitting to reveal mysteries connected with that which is above and that which is below." Thus we learn that the Torah is a code. The Torah conceals. *The Zohar* further declares:

Now there is no work of the Holy One so recondite but he has recorded it in the Torah. And the Torah has revealed it in an instant. Then straightaway clothes it with another garment so that it is hidden there and does not show itself. But the wise whose wisdom makes them full of eyes peers through the garment to the very essence of the word that is hidden nearby. And when the word is momentarily revealed in that first instant of which we have spoken, those whose eyes are wise can see it, though it is so soon hidden again.

Hebrew is not just a language intended for kabbalistic conversation. To the contrary, each of its words is a vessel of power and energy. Even when it is translated into English, much of its meaning remains. We read in *The Zohar*:

> And the letter Beth came before The Creator and said, "My Lord, I find it best for you to create within me this entire world because within me the entire world will be blessed, both the upper and the lower world, for the letter Beth signifies blessing." And the Holy One answered and said, "For surely through you I shall create the world and you shall be the beginning of creation and within you shall be the entire creation."

To be sure, it is difficult to understand how a letter—even a Hebrew one—can be a vehicle for the creation of an entire world. But one need only look at a seed to determine whether it is the seed of a man or that of an apple tree. When we plant either of these seeds, the effects will be both vast and profoundly different.

Of all the experiences we have had over the years, and of all the thoughts that have filled our minds, what remains? Usually only a fleeting recollection—a seed. And only by virtue of this seed are we aware that we have gone through any sort of experience at all. Yet through those experiences, lessons drawn are indelibly etched into our consciousness.

Have you ever wondered how it is that you can grasp the ideas conveyed by the printed word? At what point in your life did you actually learn about word meaning and sentence structure? Actually, the specific moments are of little consequence. The important fact is that you can read.

In a similar manner, the average person is acutely aware that if he puts his finger into an electrical socket, he will get a shock. Chances are that he has long since forgotten whatever experience it was—however vivid it may have been at the time—that originally taught him this lesson. Yet he need not recall the experience itself so long as the underlying lesson remains. This point holds true with regard to virtually every facet of one's personality. Just as we have learned not to jeopardize our fingers by placing them in electrical sockets, so too have we learned not to lie or cheat or steal. We may have had to learn and relearn some of these lessons in order to make them part of us, but if the lessons remain, the means by which they were initially acquired is immaterial.

The same principle holds true for reincarnation. To infer that past lives never existed simply because we have no memory of them is like contending that radio waves do not exist because they cannot be seen. The recollection of past incarnations may not lie at our fingertips, but those lives are nonetheless there. To access them, we need only reconfigure the memory banks of our metaphysical computers. With memory restored, we can recall and understand our past incarnations and thus clarify and explain our present one.

We have lost our ability to see things as they really are, and with that loss has gone our ability to become fully acquainted with our past lives. As a result, we plunge blindly through our present life using information gained in the past without the slightest awareness that we are applying it.

If heredity were the only key to human behavior, identical twins would behave in an identical fashion. Yet in any given set of twins, one may turn to art and the other to mathematics. Or perhaps one twin might be lazy while the other cannot be constrained. It is these differences that lead one to question the impact of heredity and that of reincarnation. Of the two, it is the latter that provides most of the answers parents have sought when, in one way or another, their children have gone astray. This information can alleviate a world of useless guilt on the part of the parents, as well as in the children themselves.

The paradox of divergence between parent and child is an ancient one. The Bible tells us, "Now these are the generations of Terah—Terah begat Abram, Nachor, and Charan." Terah, then, was the father of Abraham; yet the sages of the *Talmud* say that Terah was an idol worshipper and a wicked man. How, then, could he have sired a son who would grow up to be the father of the Israelite nation? Abraham was so pure and wonderful, so intelligent and enlightened, that he learned to combine the physical world with the metaphysical world and operate in each—a feat accomplished by only six of those who followed him: Isaac, Jacob, Joseph, Moses, Aaron, and David. How could a man like Terah be the forerunner of such a lineage?

The Torah provides an answer to this mystery in its description of Jacob and Esau even as they grew in Rebecca's womb:

> And the children struggled together within her and she said, "If it be so, why am I thus?"

And she went to inquire of the Lord. And the Lord said unto her, "Two nations are in thy womb, and two manners of people shall be separated from thy bowels and the one people shall be stronger than the other people and the elder shall serve the younger." And when her days to be delivered were fulfilled, behold there were twins in her womb.

This tale of Rebecca is a code that conceals the innermost secrets of our universe in general and of humanity in particular. It clarifies that all-too-common family dynamic in which two brothers hate each other, a son hates his father, a mother and daughter are at odds, or—as in the case of Terah and Abraham—there seems to be no connection at all between parent and offspring. The probability in such cases is that the two individuals in question are in no way related. Instead, they are merely acting out a vendetta that was begun in a past life, to be carried over for its conclusion in this one.

To many whose lives are dreary and difficult, the soul's desire for growth might seem inconceivable. But it is only satiety that brings about a lack of desire. Thus, an end to the cycle of reincarnation can be expected only when the soul has grown to a point at which it no longer has a desire for rebirth. Our waking consciousness is only a portion of our actual consciousness. Our deeper selves often recognize needs that our everyday consciousness overlooks.

15

THE PURPOSE OF
REINCARNATION

There are many schools of thought concerning the purpose of reincarnation. That it is for improvement of the soul is obvious, but there may be other reasons for it as well, including the soul's inherent desire for expansion and growth. Perhaps experience is the driving force that brings us back. Or perhaps learning something begets the desire to learn more, and learning more begets the desire to learn everything there is to know.

Kabbalah teaches us that just the opposite is the case. The soul resists rebirth. The soul is a metaphysical force that creates life within a physical body. But the soul earnestly desires to remain in its pure state of consciousness without having to descend to physical existence in a human form, with all the limitations that implies.

When we speak of the body and of the soul, we are not speaking only of two physical energies. The body is a physical entity, but there is a motivating force within it—something that lies beyond the workings of the cells and genetic makeup that cause it to grow and function. That force is called body energy, which can be defined as the Desire to Receive for Oneself Alone. This force is nothing less than the root of all evil. Body energy is the same as the energy of the earth, which, with the grip of its gravity, seeks to swallow everything within its reach. The body is forever attempting to revert back to the earth, which is its true home.

Only the soul provides a force that can transform the Desire to Receive for Oneself Alone into the Desire to Receive for the Purpose of Sharing. When that transformation occurs, the soul has fulfilled its destiny by having balanced its tikune, and the body dies. In a truly righteous person, body energy and soul energy become indistinguishable, and disintegration of the body is no longer necessary. In most people, however, the body must disintegrate. As long as the body exists, it can maintain its hold on the soul, which has perhaps earned its release.

As a metaphysical entity, the soul—whether it has achieved correction or not—has no inherent desire to dwell in a physical body or in the material world. The soul naturally and inevitably wishes to depart.

The soul's view of the world is anchored in a Desire to Receive for the Purpose of Sharing, and this view expresses itself as the goodness found to a greater or lesser extent in every human being. The body, however, exists solely to receive for itself alone. It eats. It drinks. It hoards. It indulges its solitary vices and shares with no one. Even the inexorable gravitational pull of the earth on which it walks feeds its desire by pulling the soul down, restricting and constraining it. Nervous or mental breakdowns, in the kabbalistic view, are nothing more than manifestations of this constant battle being waged between the body's Desire to Receive and the soul's yearning to share. When the body overwhelms the soul, it shuts off the flow of positive energy without which the soul cannot survive. The impulse toward suicide can thus be expressed in a single sentence: "I can't take it." When the soul can no longer "take" what life has to give on its own terms, it must depart.

From this principle we can gain insight into some seemingly mysterious life functions. Consider, for example, the gift of sleep. Who could survive without it? During the hours of somnolence, the soul leaves the body, returning to its origin in order to be recharged for the continuing struggle that will resume when sleep is done. Without sleep, the body would destroy the soul in short order.

This point need not be proven through metaphysical argument, for it has been borne out both in scientific experiment and in everyday human experience. People who deliberately submit themselves to sleep deprivation often begin to hallucinate. Their emotions become frenzied. Their physical coordination vanishes. Similarly, those who suffer from insomnia find themselves exhausted even though they have remained in bed eight hours each night.

Kabbalah teaches that the real problem here is less a question of sleep deprivation than of dream deprivation. Dreams are manifestations of cosmic consciousness in which knowledge exists free of the body's greed. Only in the cosmic realm of sleep can the soul receive the periodic recharging it needs. And as this takes place—as the soul roams freely out-

side the constraints of time, space, and motion—it frequently relives past incarnations, often converting these events
into revelatory dream symbols.

As it enters the body, the soul is like a man who has
been condemned to prison. It is confined, unable to exert
influence as it might desire. It is bound to conform to the
laws and principles of the physical universe just as a prisoner
must adhere to the rules of the prison. But only in the confinement of the physical world can the soul complete its
tikune, thereby earning its eternal reward in the upper world,
in the presence of its Creator.

16

FREE WILL

One of the fundamental principles of Kabbalah is a condition known as "Bread of Shame." Long before there were any stars or planets or galaxies, we all ate of this bread in the Endless World, at the time our souls were created.

Our souls were created for one reason only. The essence of The Creator is the desire to give and to share. But when The Creator existed alone, no sharing could take place. There were no Vessels to hold The Creator's endless Light— so with nothing more than desire, He created those Vessels. These are our souls to this day, and their essence is the Desire to Receive from His exalted Light.

For ages beyond our comprehension, our souls did just that. They received, and they did so with no motive other than to receive for themselves alone. But as they were filled, a new yearning evolved. Suddenly, in emulation of The Creator, our souls developed a Desire to Receive for the

Purpose of Sharing. But they were then faced with the same dilemma as that which The Creator Himself faced before He created his Vessels: With every soul filled, there was no one and nothing with whom to share.

Thus arose Bread of Shame: shame at receiving so much and giving nothing in return. Shame at having no opportunity to say "yes" or "no" to The Creator and, through that exercise of free will, prove oneself worthy to receive—and in this way dispel the Bread of Shame.

Shame led to rebellion—a mass rejection of The Creator's beneficence. When that happened, the Light was withdrawn and the material universe was created, including physical bodies desiring only to receive for themselves alone. Our souls reside in these bodies, forever struggling against body energy.

The soul, therefore, desires a sojourn in this world, not for experience or education, but rather to gain a position of choice—to be able to say to The Creator, "I have a Desire to Receive either for Myself Alone or for the Purpose of Sharing, and I can exercise either option as I choose." When we choose to selfishly exercise the body's desire, we cut off all beneficence from The Creator—but at least the choice is ours.

In the Endless World, the soul had no choice to make and no opportunity to share, since all the Vessels were full. In this world, however, there are many others with whom to share or not to share as we so choose. Learning to make the positive choice is the soul's mission in life—and it continues to be so in life after life after life, depending on the soul's degree of progress toward that goal.

There is nothing automatic about real sharing. To the contrary, it can be accomplished only through free and conscious will. If money from your account is transferred to some charitable organization through an error on the part of your bank, you can't really claim to have been a philanthropist. In order to give up part of your wealth—to share it—you must retain full control. You have an opportunity to say, "I'll give some to somebody else," or, conversely, "I'll keep it all for myself."

This concept lies at the heart of Kabbalah. It is not a matter of putting faith in God, but of putting faith in a system that teaches us how to receive for the purpose of sharing.

We, not fate, dictate every event of our lives. Negative influences—which all of us encounter at one time or another—are not a cause for despair but rather a warning to tread cautiously and avoid unnecessary risk during a dangerous period. But we are always in control. When pain, suffering, and tragedy attend us, it is only because we have mandated them in a previous incarnation and must now remove the obstacles they present so that our souls can progress. There is no such thing as "punishment" in the *tikune* process. The only purpose of that process is to move a soul toward purification.

Our present lifetime is only one station on the way. From a broad perspective, 70 or 80 or even 120 years on this earth represent but the wink of an eye. Remember that the only reason for a soul's sojourn on this earth is to earn the right to receive Light from The Creator. That right is rarely earned in the course of a single lifetime.

17

METAPHYSICAL CIRCUITRY

Whenever we receive with the intention of sharing, we reject part of what is received, thereby creating resistance. When The Creator's Light was first rejected in the Endless World, the Light withdrew—not in the sense of movement, for The Creator's Light is a constant that never moves, but in the sense that there was no Vessel to reveal the Light. If a room is dark in a house that is wired with electricity, darkness persists only because no one has thrown a switch to complete the electrical circuit. The light is always there, waiting to be revealed.

All souls have a single, common purpose when they enter this world: They are here to create Vessels that will reveal the Light. The energy is already within us—but until it is revealed, we remain unfulfilled.

We can create the necessary circuit of energy only when resistance is present. This resistance factor—whether in an electrical circuit or in a soul—creates the returning light from the positive pole, which in turn creates possibility of acceptance. The creation of Vessels is accomplished when we freely choose to act in accordance with the precepts of *The Bible*, and the metaphysical energy revealed through our actions accomplishes the *tikune* for which we have come into this world.

We are here for no other purpose than to receive the fulfillment of the Light. We seek fulfillment now because, burdened by Bread of Shame, we refused it in the Endless World at the time of creation. The degree of our desire to receive it now is the only difference that distinguishes one soul from another.

Unfortunately, all established religions preach the effect without seeking the purpose. They seek to tell their followers what to do without telling them why they should do it. They direct their adherents to be "good"—but if someone asks why, the only answer is, "Because it's in *The Bible*." But why is it in *The Bible*, and what does *The Bible* have to say to each individual soul regarding its own particular need? Established religions answer in generalities but overlook the key universal truth that applies to all humanity: Each and every one of us is a communication system whose purpose is to draw metaphysical energy from The Creator, thereby fulfilling The Creator's desire to share.

Like any circuitry, we must complete our energy circuit by means of positive, negative, and central columns. This is the system that was lost to us in the Endless World. The need to regain that system within our individual souls is what keeps us coming back to this earth plane again and again.

In the Endless World, the Vessel and the Light were equal: The Light initiated action, and the Vessel created equal and opposite reaction. Yet there was one difference between them: The Light created the Vessel, but the Vessel did not create another Vessel. The Light created a Vessel with which to share of itself. The Vessel, which was merely the recipient of this action, could not create on its own.

Bread of Shame was the result of this inability to create. The Vessels—all the souls in creation—in effect said to The Creator, "No—you can use us as Vessels only if we can create a Vessel that will reveal you. In this way we will be able to share with you, even as you share with us."

God created man in His own image because man, in the Endless World, demanded it. He said, "I want to be as close to you as possible. And I am close to you in all respects save this: I am the Vessel you created to reveal yourself. But Bread of Shame forbids that I continue to reveal you until I myself can create the Vessel whereby this is accomplished."

But why, if oneness with God was humanity's first desire, do we so often commit crimes and perpetrate acts of violence of every possible description? And why have we done so since the beginning of time? Why will even the best among us, if they are honest, admit to having shocking thoughts and intentions?

The reason is simple: Each of us must have the opportunity to say no.

In the absence of conscience or morality, killing a competitor in business, to offer but one example, might make perfectly good sense. After all, if a businessman eliminates a

competitor, he will make more money, will he not? He will
have taken a life but will have gained greater profits.

Kabbalah teaches that there can be no such thing as
murder for gain, simply because gain can never result from
murder. In the Endless World, we existed as Vessels whose
sole function was to reveal The Creator by receiving His
Light. But that system existed only until Bread of Shame
caused us to reject God's beneficence—by refusing to receive
unless we could create and share with a Vessel of our own.

Killing involves taking another's energy without first
creating a Vessel in which to hold that energy. And the only
way in which we can create such a Vessel is to reject killing.
Without a Vessel, a human being can never hold onto whatever gain an act of murder might bring. Any energy thus
taken remains with the murderer until, in either the present
lifetime or a future one, a Vessel is created to contain that
energy and relieve him of his burden.

Inherited wealth is subject to the same principle.
Without charity—without the creation of a Vessel through
an act of sharing—the energy of inherited wealth cannot be
retained. This is not to say that an inherited fortune is com-
parable to money gained through an act of violence. But an
inheritance also involves Bread of Shame to the extent that it
does nothing more than serve the Desire to Receive for
Oneself Alone. Bread of Shame whispers, "Look at all the
potential energy of that money. It's not really yours, and having that money does not make you any better than the person who has no money."

If we are to truly gain ownership of this energy, we
must establish companionship, friendship, and intimacy with

our fellow human beings. Only through this connection can a Desire to Receive for the Purpose of Sharing be established. The recipient of an inheritance cannot fulfill his soul with money, for the soul does not need money. It needs only internal energy, and it can gain that internal energy by giving and sharing the money. It is for this reason that *The Bible* commands us to give away a tithe amounting to 10% of our yearly earnings. By doing so freely and joyfully, we create the Vessel with which to contain and maintain the other 90% of our earnings.

18

THE DIVINE EQUITY

There are circumstances under which a soul returns to this earth plane solely for the purpose of helping someone else grow and fulfill the purpose of his or her incarnation. At times the returning soul will even accomplish that mission by creating misery. In this way, a situation that existed in a prior lifetime will have been re-created. The soul that is being tested is then given the opportunity to make a new choice as to how it will behave.

It is possible that a soul who is being unkind to another is doing so because the other soul had been unkind to him in a prior lifetime. Thus, a murder victim is never really a "victim" from the perspective of reincarnation. Invariably, the "victim" committed murder in a prior lifetime and is now making the necessary correction.

The death of a child provides yet another example in which a soul causes pain to others for the sake of growth and correction. Returning to pay back debts incurred in a prior lifetime does not apply to a child under the age of 13. But if a child dies at such an early age, it is possible that he was here only to create necessary anguish for the people who are his parents. Through that anguish, the parents can correct a problem they incurred in this or a prior lifetime. Any soul that lives in the body past the age of 13 is here for its own tikune. Prior to that, it is here only to set a stage.

If we cannot see how the death of a child has affected the spiritual condition of the grief-stricken parents, it is only because of our own limited insight and understanding. Above all else, the laws of *tikune* can be understood only through the tools and teachings of Kabbalah. Tikune, which operates on a mental and moral plane, is a principle of cause and effect. The law of *tikune* decrees that for every action there must be an equal and corresponding reaction—so that ultimately we all receive exactly what we have "asked for."

There is a proverb that states, "Cast thy bread upon the waters, for thou shalt find it after many days." If people could accept the truth of this proverb, the world would be a different place. Simply put, this adage signifies that the practice of goodness and kindness will be rewarded unexpectedly after a long interval. It means that whatever we plant is what we will reap. A universal understanding of this, the law of tikune, could transform the entire world.

If people really accepted this principle, "love thy neighbor" would be regarded as a practical rule of life rather than as a remote concept or an abstract ideal. We would know that the only thing we can take with us beyond the grave is what we have given away.

A modern bank provides an excellent analogy for this teaching. When a person takes out a loan from the bank, it is understood that he must repay that loan. In effect, he has taken something that doesn't belong to him—something that he has not yet earned. In keeping with the law of cause and effect as well as that of action and reaction, repayment must follow.

If, like the bank customer, we take something in this life with the expectation of ultimately paying for it, we must still operate under the law of tikune. A single incarnation, however, may not provide the occasion and opportunity for an individual to receive what he has earned. Nor will it necessarily provide time for the payment of a credit that has been extended.

When we refer to a "short circuit" in kabbalistic terms, we speak of someone who has received energy without removing his Bread of Shame. We are, in effect, saying that he has gone through a life without repaying what he has received. To be sure, he may have been paid for all the good he has done in this lifetime, but he has not paid for all the evil he has perpetrated. That is why we frequently encounter people who are enjoying success and good fortune despite the fact that they obviously have not earned it. We must remember that this life is only one chapter in a very long book. In a subsequent incarnation, they will pay for their evil in full.

Adolf Eichmann, who was ultimately seized for his crimes and tried in Israel years after World War II had ended, defended his heinous actions with the excuse, "I was only following orders." Lieutenant Calley said the same thing of the massacre he led at My Lai village in Vietnam. Kabbalistically speaking, we must lay aside our outrage at these statements. Instead, we must ask why those two souls were placed in a position to decide whether or not they should follow such orders. The respective roles of these two men—one a German Nazi, the other an American officer— were clearly roles of massive tikune. Most cases are not so obvious.

As we move into the Age of Aquarius, we find very few souls among us that have not been incarnated at one time or another. In a prior lifetime, perhaps someone was a bank robber whose actions led to many deaths. In this lifetime, he may be a famous surgeon who uses his skill to save lives. If this individual can escape the built-in ego traps inherent in such a situation, realizing all the while that his skill is only a tool and not a manifestation of his own glory, he may be able to correct the evil he wrought in a prior lifetime.

Unfortunately, it usually takes many lifetimes to complete a tikune. This would not be the case if we grasped the problem and applied ourselves to it rather than dwelling in unhappiness over some imagined injustice. We usually avoid taking advantage of lessons taught in our daily lives until such time as we are forced by bitter experience to examine them. Generally, these lessons must be patiently repeated day after day, year after year, even lifetime after lifetime— until the knowledge we have so persistently ignored comes crashing in on us, sometimes in a most devastating fashion. If we could learn to cooperate with the universe rather than stubbornly resisting it, our spiritual growth would flourish.

19

STRUCTURE OF THE SOUL

The desire to receive for the self alone is a universal tendency. But this selfishness is a distortion and a warped reflection of the Light we are here to receive. Kabbalah teaches that before a person can know and abide by the laws of tikune, he must know the root and place of his soul.

To know that, however, we must first understand the structure within which root and place are found. Like so much in the world of metaphysics, that structure is a triad. It consists of *Nefesh*, which is the realm of crude spirit; *Ruah*, which is the realm of spirit more refined; and *Neshamah*, which is the realm of the true soul.

The soul within the realm of *Nefesh* is more closely aligned with body energy and is materialistic in nature. It is the consciousness of never having enough, and of insensitivity to the needs and desires of others.

Through the process of tikune, a soul may eventually reach the level of *Ruah*, in which it still experiences hungers and desires but is no longer ruled by them. Certain wants are bypassed because they can be fulfilled only at the expense of others. The soul at the level of *Ruah* is fertile ground for the first green growth of true charity.

Neshamah is at the top of the spiritual triad. The inherent desire to receive is still present, but it is totally subordinate to the desire to share.

There is rarely any mystery as to what level a specific soul has attained, because the soul's characteristics are quickly expressed in the actions of the individual. For most of us, life is a struggle to move beyond self-centered *Nefesh*, to pass through *Ruah*, and ultimately to achieve *Neshamah*.

The Zohar says, "Praiseworthy are those who indulge in the Torah to know the wisdom of their law, and furthermore they know and reflect upon the upper internal secrets when they leave this world. For through death and repentance, the harsh judgment of this world is removed."

It is through reflection that we come to know the laws of the universe as well as to know ourselves. By understanding the law of tikune, we come to know how we will have to present an account of our deeds before The Creator. We must also know and reflect on the secrets of *The Zohar*. Why has a soul come into this particular body? Why has this body received the grade of soul that occupies it? On what foundation does this world stand? How must one share in its correction?

The Song of Songs says, "Tell me, O thou whom my soul loves, where thou makest thy flock to rest at noon." *The*

Zohar explains that this is the soul speaking to The Creator, saying, "Tell me the mysteries of the supernal wisdom. How do you lead your flock in the upper world? Teach me some of the mysteries of the wisdom, for I have not learned them. Teach me so I will not be in shame when I come to be among the eternal souls, for until now I have not reflected on these mysteries."

The Song of Songs continues with the response of The Creator: "If thou knowest not, oh thou fairest of women, go thy way forth by the footsteps of the flock, and feed thy lambs beside the shepherds' tents." *The Zohar* interprets this passage as follows: "If you do not understand the beauty of the soul, if you come to the upper world and haven't reflected upon the soul's mysteries, then you will not merit entrance. Therefore return again. Learn those things that, in your previous life, you considered to be unimportant, and you shall be worthy to reside in the upper world forever."

We have all heard the expression "Out of the mouth of babes comes wisdom," but few really know its meaning. When *the Song of Songs* instructs us to "feed thy lambs beside the shepherds' tents," it is referring to the places where children learn. They are only children, but if we listen carefully, we will hear many of the secrets of reincarnation.

From a kabbalistic standpoint, all forms of pain, suffering, illness, and injury have their origins in *tikune* and are there to promote spiritual growth. At the same time, *tikune* itself must not be fatalistically interpreted. We cannot escape the results of past actions, but we can change those results by what we do now. How can this be accomplished? By allowing the soul to become aware of its defects and to correct itself by bringing itself into alignment with the forces of the universe.

This is not to say that we should ignore people who are suffering on the grounds that they are merely working off their tikune. While it is not our duty to interfere with the process, we can look upon the sufferer in a different light and help him bear his burden without trying to bear it for him. With the tools and teachings of Kabbalah, we can project ourselves backward in time to see these individuals in a different condition of the soul. And in so doing, we can help them ascertain the true source of their difficulty.

Before we conclude this discussion of tikune, let us clarify how people can be held individually responsible for the customs and obligations of their time. If the society of the Middle Ages called on people to do things that would today be considered immoral and illegal, to what extent are those individuals accountable?

The answer to this seemingly complex problem is, quite simply, that it depends on your frame of reference. There is an old joke in which someone greets a friend with the standard pleasantry, "How are you?" The perceptive friend answers, "Compared to what?"

In the biblical Book of *Numbers*, God commanded Moses to speak to a stone that it might bring forth water. But Moses was angry and struck the stone. Although the result was the same—the water emerged from the stone—Moses forever surrendered his right to enter the Promised Land by virtue of his momentary loss of control. An observer might legitimately complain that the penalty Moses incurred was out of proportion to his transgression—and from the observer's frame of reference, this would be true. But Moses, who had communed directly with The Creator, lived in a different frame of reference—and only within that framework could his actions be understood.

A man might say of a previous life, "I was a very pious religious leader." But neither his piety nor his works have meaning outside the frame of reference in which he applied them. An individual might appear to be a saint, yet that same individual might be light years away from fulfilling the *tikune* he bears. When the *Talmud* tells us, "Judge not your friend until you reach his station," it is really saying that we are incapable of judging until we know the frame of reference in which that friend dwells.

In the entire universe, there is no such thing as an accident. All misfortunes or "accidents" encountered in the present are merely the logical outgrowth of some action that was taken either in a past life or in the present one. Misfortune and illness are merely the effects of causative factors operating under the laws of tikune. Therefore, anyone who suffers some form of injury or illness should immediately ask himself whether it is the result of a *tikune* condition from a past incarnation or the consequence of some flaw in his present lifetime. The illness itself might be nothing more than the result of having eaten, drunk, or smoked too much, but the need some people feel to overindulge invariably has its origins in tikune.

Kabbalah teaches us that the soul is part of God, and that the part is one with the whole. The only difference is that the soul is the part, and God is the complete universal spirit. When we speak of the laws of tikune, we must there-

fore understand that there is a cosmic spiritual energy that
can help us change or remove any misfortune that has befall-
en us.

20

REINCARNATION AND MARRIAGE

While infinitely rewarding at its best, the experience of marriage can be unspeakably oppressive at its worst. Marriage offers the utmost extremes of human happiness and human bondage, with all the lesser degrees in between.

Legally, marriage is a contract. Psychologically, it can be regarded as a theater of sexual and emotional drama. kabbalistic traditional law regards it as a sacrament, as does Christian doctrine. The cynic sees it as a trap for fools, saying, quite truthfully, that the best way to kill a romance is to get married.

All of these viewpoints may have validity, but according to the more comprehensive perspective provided by the reincarnation principle, it would be wrong to accept any of them as the ultimate truth. According to kabbalistic teachings, marriage is an opportunity for two imperfect individuals to help each other discharge their respective *tikune* debts and advance their spiritual understanding. No marriage is a result of chance, and none is begun on a clean slate. Every marriage is an episode in a series of stories begun long ago, in previous lives.

The Zohar clearly states, "Note that all the figures of souls that are to be born stand before the Almighty in pairs." Put another way, souls are divided into male and female— and after they have worked their way through the corridors of reincarnation and have gained correction sufficient to merit one another, the Almighty brings them back together.

There is no bliss in the physical universe greater than that of reunification. But it must be earned by soul growth over many lifetimes, during which time marriage may prove to be anything but bliss.

Soulmates are the two halves—male and female—of what began in the Endless World as a single soul, divided by the hand of the Almighty in preparation for the long trek through this world. Only when *tikune* has been accomplished and karmic debts have been discharged can these two halves come together again on this plane. But no marriage is a mistake. Although partners may be very far from soulmates, they can still help each other move toward the spiritual state in which reunion with the soulmate has been fully earned.

The majority of women accomplish *tikune* much more quickly than do men. Most women, in fact, are here in the world simply to help men bear their karmic burdens. When a woman is seen to be especially hard on her husband, it is usually an indication that she is doing precisely what she should be doing to help him make his tikune.

Scripture tells us there is nothing new under the sun—and certainly the wedding of soulmates is no exception, since their joining has long since taken place in the upper world. Soulmates were promised to each other from the beginning. As the kabbalists put it, "Happy are the righteous whose souls are beautified before the holy king before they come into this world." When the time comes for soulmates to marry, the Almighty, who knows each spirit and soul, rejoins them as they were at first and proclaims their union.

But only if a man has led a virtuous life is he privileged to marry his true soulmate. Indeed, there are times when a woman will be reincarnated specifically for the opportunity to marry her soulmate, because he may not have merited it in prior lifetimes.

Even after winning his soulmate, however, a man remains vulnerable. If he then leads an extremely sinful life, he may have to return to this world without his soulmate for the purpose of tikune. This point is made clear in *The Zohar*, which states, "If he shall enter into slavery by himself, by himself shall he go out." On the surface, this passage would appear to represent but one of several verses addressing the treatment of slaves. In fact, however, it refers to an individual who has failed, in a given incarnation, to merit union with his soulmate.

Difficulty can also arise when a good man merits, if not his soulmate, at least a good woman—only to lose her when she encounters her true soulmate, who merits her as well.

When soulmates meet and marry, knowingly or otherwise, they have agreed to costar once more with someone they have known in one or more previous lifetimes. At any

time, the players can alter the promise of the plot; although
the stage has been set, the lines have not necessarily been
written. As a result, even if two people are soulmates, they
may still encounter problems if they fail to understand the
principles of reincarnation. Through lack of understanding,
they can plunge themselves unnecessarily into the maelstrom
of infidelity and divorce. Many a good marriage goes on the
rocks solely out of ignorance of the reincarnation process.
Sociologists and psychologists generally try to explain marital infidelity as a biological phenomenon, but from a kabbalistic standpoint, *tikune* is far more likely to lie at the root of
the problem.

In every society, marriage takes place through a carefully performed ceremony. Even civil marriages require the
pronouncement of certain lines and the taking of certain
vows. These ceremonies and vows have served mankind since
the beginning of human history—yet increasing numbers of
young people today are casting them aside. "We love each
other," they proclaim, "so why do we need a piece of paper
to prove it?" The answer is simple: Rituals, rules, and regu-
lations are what make marriage an institution, and abandon-
ing them promotes total disregard for the sanctity of the
union between a man and a woman. Without the middle-col-
umn force of that sanctity, short-circuiting becomes almost
inevitable.

This short-circuiting damages far more than the marriage in question. In fact, it wreaks havoc on the universe as
a whole, because it becomes a primary source of negativity.
Most human beings are "sitting on the fence" from a spiritual perspective: They are neither particularly good nor partic-

ularly bad. For them, the balance is easily tipped. An abundance of negativity—including the effect of marital strife, even if it is not their own—can lead people to behave in a negative fashion.

Our objective in any given lifetime is to convert our inherent Desire to Receive into a Desire to Share. Only when this has been accomplished can we create a circuit. Thus, the purpose of repentance is not simply to say, "I'm sorry." It is to restore whatever positive energy has been taken away on both the micro and macro levels. As an individual self is affected, so too is the entire universe. Ritual, therefore, is not empty posturing. It is a metaphysical system under which positive energy is infused—or, if necessary, restored.

A wise adage says, "Marriage is like a besieged fortress—those who are outside want to get in and those who are inside want to get out." When we look at most marriages, with the misery they seem to engender for both husband and wife, it is surprising that anyone would find this to be a desirable state. Nonetheless, the unmarried generally have a strong feeling of having been cheated out of something precious in their free but solitary lives. And in point of fact, they are quite correct.

21

Discovering Your Soulmate

In this chapter, we shall explore the origin of soulmates and the methodology by which one can discover one's own soulmate.

There can be little doubt that one of the most intimate and complex of human relationships is that of marriage. Immensely rewarding at its best but exceedingly depressing at its worst, marriage offers up the extremes of individual happiness and human bondage—with greater or lesser degrees of each in between.

Are both extremes predestined? Must one partner discover the joy of marriage while the other experiences only the tragedy of this institution? On what conditions, if any, are these circumstances based? When is marriage advisable or inadvisable? Is it possible to determine in advance whether there is anyone else with whom one could be as happy as— or even happier than—one will be with one's intended spouse?

It is probably safe to assume that most marriages result largely from an irresistible physical attraction. This goes far toward explaining the high divorce rate in our modern society—for a successful marriage must also be rooted in an understanding of the reincarnation process. One should, in other words, be well mated not only physically but also spiritually. However, before I provide some clues that can prevent one from thoughtlessly entering into marriage, let us first investigate the primal framework of soulmates.

The doctrine of the soul, as expounded by the author of *The Zohar*, sheds considerable light on the subject of soulmates. *The Zohar* teaches that all souls have existed since the beginning of creation. Indeed, *The Zohar* goes so far as to assert that these preexisting souls were already preformed in their full individual intelligence while they were still hidden within the womb of eternity.

When The Creator made the world, all the souls of the righteous were concealed in the divine idea, each in its peculiar form. When He shaped the world, the souls were actualized and stood before him. Strange as it may seem, the concept of extraterrestrial intelligence was first articulated in *The Zohar*.

The idea that souls are essentially intelligent energy forces has finally taken root, largely because of the profound interest that modern scientists have demonstrated in it. To be sure, the idea is natural enough. It has certainly occurred to anyone who has contemplated the question of intelligent life in the universe. According to *The Zohar*, these intelligent life forces existed long before creation. In fact, souls are nothing more than varying degrees of the Desire to Receive, created in the Endless World. Rav Ashlag stresses the idea that all life forms are nothing more than aspects of intelligent energy forces. Desire is intelligence.

What took place after these forces became actualized? How did these life intelligences become manifest in our universe? *The Zohar* offers a precise description of the ultimate physical expression of these metaphysical intelligent beings:

> When the soul is about to descend to this world, it first goes down to the terrestrial Garden of Eden and sees there the glory of the souls of the righteous, and then it goes down to *Gehinnom* [Hell] and sees the wicked who cry "Woe, woe," and find no compassion. That holy form [the internal energy force] stands by him until he emerges into this world, after which it keeps him company and grows up with him. All initial souls are compounded of male and female. When they go forth into the terrestrial world, the initial soul is divided into two separate entities; the two elements are separated. The intelligent life forces of the male function become clothed in a male corporeality and the female intelligent life force in a female corporeal body. If the man has achieved a level of spiritual consciousness, both male and female intelligent forces will again become united as one harmonious unit. The male has found his soulmate. It is then that he truly meets his mate and there is a perfect union both in spirit and flesh. But if he

is not worthy, she is given to another, and they
bear children whom they should not.

Herein lies the secret of the soul's yearning: its true
soulmate, whose identity and whereabouts will become
known only when the male has achieved a particular level of
spirituality or altered state of consciousness. The male soul
desires to be reunited with his female counterpart, for only
then does the initial soul succeed in returning to its original
state of wholeness. The female soul is already endowed with
the level of consciousness of Binah and consequently does
not have to strive for a higher level for this purpose.

This information somehow appears to surface within
the conscious mind during the state of spiritual elevation. In
one of his discussions with his teacher, Rav Isaac Luria, Rav
Chaim Vital was told the following:

> My soul was spiritually superior to that of
> some of the most exalted supernal angels, and . . .
> I could achieve a much higher level of altered
> states of consciousness. When questioning the
> Ari as to my incarnated soul, he replied, "Your
> soul is that of Don Vidal de Tolosa [a Spanish rav
> and commentator on Maimonides who lived in
> the second half of the 14th century]. The reason
> for my reincarnation is to correct [tikune] and
> amend the disbelief I had in the wisdom of The
> Zohar." From the words of the Ari I understood
> that in my prior lifetime I had a deep and pene-
> trating mind. During my present sojourn, I am

very lax in making use of my innate ability, that of deep penetration.

Insofar as my present wife Hanna is concerned, she is a reincarnation of Rav Akiva's father-in-law, Kalba Savu'a, one of the wealthiest men in Jerusalem. The latter's opposition to his daughter Rachel's marriage to Akiva led him to cut them both off. Abandoned to extreme poverty, Rachel once even sold her hair for food. Rachel made her marriage to Akiva conditional upon his devoting himself to Torah study.

The reason for my present wife is that the soul of Rav Akiva and mine are of one origin. He is closer to me than all other incarnated souls within me. And because Kalba Savu'a was a homosexual, he returned as a woman. And because her [Hannah's] incarnation is one of a male, there is absolutely no possibility for her to give birth to sons. Regarding to her giving birth to girls, this is also impossible unless another female soul become incarnated within Hannah.

However, the Ari continued, Hannah will die. And when I [Chaim Vital] shall achieve the level of *Ruah*, the same altered state of consciousness of Rav Akiva, I shall then merit my soulmate. She will be Rachel, the faithful wife of Rav Akiva. And from this marriage shall come

forth your faithful son, Shmuel, who shall set
down all my writings. You will then merit worthy children.

What seems to emerge from the passage cited above is
the critical need for the male to achieve an altered state of
consciousness. This in turn sets the stage for the birth of
children with a more highly elevated level of spirituality. The
soulmate (female) must therefore be sought out so that patterns of *tikune* can be fruitfully played out. The separation of
the sexes, which comes about as souls prepare to enter the
terrestrial realm, provides an opportunity for each entity to
experience the testing of earth's proving grounds. It is the
male entity that will ultimately earn the right to a reunion
with his divine other half. And it is with the faithful soulmate
that we shall finally share complete fulfillment. In the
reunion of male and female, the ultimate circuit of intelligent
energy will have come about—and along with it the realiza-
tion of a fulfillment beyond anything that we might ever
experience here on earth.

It is precisely this yearning that gives us an opportunity to learn that love is not emotion or passion alone. In time
we begin to understand that love is neither self-satisfaction
nor, initially, sex. Within this seeking process we may
encounter our soulmates over and over again; perhaps they
may appear as parents, sisters, lovers, children, or even ene-
mies. The particular relationship in any given reincarnation
is a learning experience that hopefully brings about correction and altered states of consciousness. Some will learn real
love through many incarnations, while others who are more

fortunate may not have to go through human bondage in their quest to find their soulmate.

But must one person find joy in marriage while another experiences tragedy? Are these frameworks of marriage predestined? The answer lies in one's search for spiritual growth. The fulfillment and joy of marriage rest completely on finding one's soulmate. And this reunion comes about through the experiencing of altered states of consciousness. Only then will the ultimate circuit of intelligent energy forces become firmly established. This in turn will pave the way for the birth of spiritually minded children, the joy of which lies beyond any material pleasure one might ever experience.

But what happens with the majority of earth-bound individuals, who have no understanding of the survival of the human spirit or of reincarnation? The chance that such individuals will find their soulmates is essentially nil. For them, the enjoyment of marriage will remain elusive. Furthermore, ignorance of the wisdom of the Kabbalah brings with it consequences that intelligent individuals will make every effort to avoid.

So just what does lie in store for those who have not yet achieved an altered state of consciousness?

Divorce is certainly the lot of many, particularly for the nonspiritual man. But does this imply that marrying a divorcée points to the circumstance of human bondage we described above? Of course not. Why, then, does this idea seem to be central to the passage we have cited? The secret revelation of yet another passage in *The Zohar* should allay any fears surrounding the marrying of a divorcée. While raising many other issues, information concerning the mystical realm of reality can serve as an invaluable tool in our quest to achieve reunion and self-fulfillment. The ultimate purpose of both the married and nonmarried states lies in the achievement of altered states of consciousness. This is probably one of the safest means of providing man with freedom of will and power of choice. One of the most important aspects of reincarnation lies in its recognition of free will. Yet an inaccurate assumption made by many who accept the *tikune* and reincarnation principle is that all of life has already been predetermined. The implications of such an assumption are mentally paralyzing.

The restrictions placed on us in our present lifetime are in fact a direct result of mistakes and errors we have made in the past. A thorough understanding of the *tikune* process, however, can resolve the ancient conflict of free will versus determinism. On a birth level of consciousness, the radius of free will is largely determined by the *tikune* process of former lifetimes. But once an individual has escaped the original state of reincarnation and has entered a higher level of spirituality, natal restrictions no longer apply. The intelligent energy force dictating and programming the metaphysical and physical DNA lies on a natal frequency. As such, once the incarnated soul has elevated itself to another level of consciousness, the printout of the natal DNA no longer applies inasmuch as former lifetime actions affect the soul on the level at which the errors and mistakes have occurred. If the level of consciousness of a particular soul was in a state of *Nefesh* at birth and in its present lifetime achieves a level of *Ruah*, we are now relating to what is essentially another per-

son, another frame of reference. Consequently, it becomes
abundantly clear that in marriage as in all else, man is completely free to do as he will; what makes the difference is the
determination to achieve altered states of consciousness.
Once this happens, a new computer printout takes over,
together with a new set of principles. A completely different
DNA structure becomes manifest, allowing for a new set of
circumstances that can result in a life of accomplishment and
fulfillment.

Let us now consider *The Zohar*'s teachings about previously married women:

> Old man, old man! If thou art to reveal
> mysteries, speak out without fear! We have said
> that the intelligence life form [the internal ener-
> gy force of the sperm] of a man is left in the
> woman who was his wife. Well, what becomes of
> it? Supposing she marries again; is it possible
> that two different life forms of two men should
> dwell together in one woman? Is the force of the
> first husband entirely lost? Nay, this cannot be.
> The same problem arises even when the widow
> does not marry again. What becomes of her hus-
> band's life form which cleaves to her? All this
> must now be explained.
>
> When the second husband's intelligence
> enters into the body of the woman, the intelli-
> gence of the first husband contends with it, and
> they cannot dwell in peace together, so that the

woman is never altogether happy with the second husband, because the intelligence force of
the first one is always pricking her, his memory
is always with her, causing her to weep and sigh
over him. In fact, his spirit writhes within her
like a serpent. And so it goes on for a long time.
If the second intelligence prevails over the first
one [that means the second union is one of soul-
mates], then the intelligence of the first husband
goes out. But if, as sometimes happens, the first
conquers the second, inasmuch as the first union
was one of soulmates, it means the death of the
second husband. Therefore, we are taught that
after a woman has been twice widowed no one
should marry her again, for the angel of death
has taken possession of her though most people
do not know this. Friends, I am aware that on
this point you may well object that in that case
the second husband's death was not in accordance with fairness by Divine Judgment. It is not
so, however. It is all decided by fair trial,
whether the one spirit should prevail over the
other or be at peace with it; but he who marries
a widow is like unto one who ventures to brave
the ocean during a storm without a rudder or
sails, and knows not whether he will cross safely
or sink into the depths.

This passage is essentially saying that ignorance of the
law, be it physical or metaphysical, is no excuse. To the con-

trary, *The Zohar* cautions that it is incumbent on all of us to understand the laws and principles governing soulmates. The price of ignorance is enormous, sometimes even causing untimely death. This startling revelation concerning the intelligence of the sperm and its unyielding energy force after the death of the first husband is far-reaching. Even more remarkable, however, is the fact that although the internal energy-intelligence of the sperm has been severed from its source—the first husband—it continues to wreak havoc on the lives of subsequent husbands. Only if the first husband was not the soulmate of this woman can the energy circuit of the second marriage—which is one of a reunited soul mating—overpower and overcome the intelligence energy of the first husband. The extraordinary thing about all this is that the wife herself may never even know why she is "never altogether happy" with her second husband. Her decision to marry again no doubt resulted from much deliberation and soul searching. Nevertheless, she was determined not to remain alone despite the fulfilling life she had led with her first husband.

Alone—there is something barren in the word. Remaining alone is perhaps the saddest phrase one can confront after losing love. Whatever the *tikune* reasons are for the woman to remain alone, the second husband should have explored the issue of soulmates more thoroughly. As spiritual incompatibility becomes more intense, divorce may seem advisable after one has considered all other factors involved—namely, level of spirituality, children, and consultation with a marriage counselor. Marriage is more serious than most people think. In the example just cited, death may come to the second husband prematurely if his investigation reveals that his present wife may already have traveled through her current lifetime with her soulmate. This is precisely the reason *The Zohar* warns that "after a woman who has been twice widowed no one should marry her again."

There is a strong possibility that in this case, the woman's first husband was her soulmate and that his intelligence was felt during the second marriage, causing the death of her second husband. If the second marriage was terminated by divorce, however, we have no real basis on which to assume that the first marriage was indeed a soul union.

3

CLUES OF SOULMATE MARRIAGES

"Should I get married? How can I be sure I am doing the right thing?" Every prospective bride or groom has posed these questions.

There can be little doubt that one of the most intimate and complex of human relationships is that of marriage. Immensely rewarding at its best but exceedingly depressing at its worst, marriage offers up the extremes of individual happiness and human bondage—with greater or lesser degrees of each in between.

To find the answers, one must first begin connecting with the real self. For if you haven't the faintest idea what really makes you tick, how can you dream of knowing the other half of yourself? If half of a soulmate is yourself but you have no a clue as to who you really are, can you presume that knowledge of your counterpart is something you can easily acquire?

Although most people are of the opinion that they enter life as new human beings, we have now seen that this is not the case. After all, is our behavior not influenced by unconscious psychological difficulties, fears, suppressed traumas, and a host of other idiosyncrasies? Where did it all come from if not from the personal experiences of former lifetimes? It appears to me that all experiences are programmed as part of an overall scheme of which we are only partially aware.

If we haven't successfully learned all there is to know about ourselves, however, what advice can Kabbalah offer to help us become consciously aware of our soulmate? Suppose the decision to become marriage partners has been made, and the details of the wedding have reached the planning stage. The date has been set, the place of the wedding ceremony chosen, and the invitations mailed. The couple now sits back and enjoys this carefree period, which may never again be theirs.

Several days before the wedding date, however, doubts begin to set in. There have been several nasty confrontations—nothing of real importance, but all serious enough to inspire second thoughts. Should we call it all off? "Perish the thought," demands the rational psyche. After all, the invitations have already been mailed out. You can't just tell all your friends and relatives not to come because you have changed your mind! Furthermore, what are you going to do about the lavish wedding reception that has been so meticulously planned? Can you imagine the embarrassment all this will cause for the parents? No! Think no more. All will be well. It's going to work out.

Did these familiar thoughts go through your mind just prior to your wedding date? Is this the kind of thinking that now makes you doubt whether you want to go through with your marriage at all?

Be prepared when entering matrimony with someone other than your soulmate. To be sure, this is not to say that there is anything wrong with doing so. Indeed, *The Zohar* seems to indicate that most marriages do take place with someone other than one's soulmate. So infrequent are soulmate marriages that *The Zohar* goes to great lengths to clarify how such marriages come about, as well as to describe the progeny that result from such unions.

When King David committed his great sin in taking Bath Sheba, he thought that it would leave its mark forever. But the message came to him, "The Lord hath put away thy sin, thou shalt not die"—which is to say that the stain had been removed.

Rav Abba put this question to Rav Shimon:

> Since we have been taught that Bath Sheba was destined for King David from the day of the creation, why did God first give her to Uriah the Hittite? R. Shimon replied: Such is the way of the Lord; although a woman is destined for a certain man, He first allows her to be the wife of another man until the time of the soulmate arrives. As soon as that time arrives, he departs from the world [he dies] to make way for the other, although the Lord is loath to remove him from the world to make way for the other man

before his time arrives. This is the inner reason
why Bath Sheba was given to Uriah first.

The Zohar's account of this most famous of all biblical
love stories is of particular interest in that it ventures far
beyond the superficial tale of two lovers. Rav Shimon reaches into the inner recesses of the soul's yearning for its true
soulmate. He defines marriage as a step by which two individuals unite their forces in the struggle to advance spiritual
understanding and to help one another discharge their
respective tikune debts. The Zohar affirms that no major
human relationship is the result of chance, but is instead a
direct result of a tikune process that was established at the
time of the world's creation. A marriage whose participants
simply cannot bear to be without each other all the time
exemplifies that of soulmates in its highest form. Such a
union is an episode in a serial begun long before. The need
to be together all the time is made necessary by the tikune
process. Thus, while Bath Sheba was married to Uriah the
Hittite, David—whose soul knew the identity and whereabouts of its soulmate—yearned to be reunited and felt a deep
need to be together again. The tikune process had governed
their separation. Now, at last, they would be united again.

But what was to become of Uriah, Bath Sheba's husband, when David reached the level of spirituality necessary
to become reunited with her? Again, The Zohar states, "As
soon as that time arrives, he departs from the world [he dies]
to make way for the other." From passages such as these, one
can deduce the principle of choice that a marriage partner
must make in the tikune process of soulmates. Uriah should

have known in advance that Bath Sheba was not his soulmate. Consequently, he should have taken the required steps to avoid his untimely death.

Divorce as laid down in *The Bible* is one of the 613 precepts that provide the individual with tools for making one's *tikune* correction. This is not to say that all males should now take this initial step and divorce their wives. To the contrary, Kabbalah emphasizes the necessity of knowing the reincarnation process—and, furthermore, of knowing just what steps one must take to avoid the pitfalls of an explosive *tikune* situation. The termination of his marriage by divorce would have prevented Uriah's untimely death. Within the *tikune* program, death for Uriah seemed inevitable. However, Uriah may have had other lessons to learn this time around—lessons that were perhaps more important than the relationship itself. Divorce would have spared his life, but he did not choose to make that decision.

The right of self-determination is seen by *The Zohar* as one of the cardinal tenets of Kabbalah. Rav Shimon considers the matter of divorce not only a moral right, but also one that is cosmically attuned to the *tikune* process of soulmates. Yet the right of man to demonstrate free will and self-determination in terminating a marriage is still rejected in many societies. Indeed, many a hostile argument has been waged over it in families affected by divorce. The consequences of such a belief are at times devastating, psychologically paralyzing and, ultimately spiritually demoralizing.

The more comprehensive worldview provided by Kabbalah will prepare the individual in his long journey through marriage. The bitter struggles that usually accompany divorce need not emerge. At the same time, knowledge of the *tikune* process and the reincarnation principle can only strengthen the already close ties that exist between true soul-mates. It is information that one can ill afford to neglect or ignore.

Regarding the matter of David and Bath Sheba, a further point must be made. Did David sin in his longing for Bath Sheba while she was still married to Uriah? What of the commandment "Thou shalt not covet thy neighbor's wife"? Did not King David himself declare, "Against thee, thee only, have I sinned, and done this evil in thy sight"?

It is in this new disclosure, at once strange and forbidden, that we encounter one of the most paradoxical of all areas covered by *The Zohar*. If Bath Sheba and David were indeed designated as soulmates at the time of creation—a marriage truly made in heaven—how could David have ignored the prohibition against coveting one's neighbor's wife? This point needs to be stressed, for it explains the depth of the reincarnation and *tikune* process. The mystical conception of the Torah is fundamental to an understanding of the paradox now facing us. *The Zohar*, employing every device of that mystical precision with which the kabbalists read *The Bible*, infused extraordinarily revealing meanings into the words of the Psalms.

King David said, "Against thee, thee only, have I sinned, and done this evil in thy sight." The significance of this statement is as follows: It is possible to commit sins that are offenses against both the Lord and man, and one can also commit sins that are offenses against man but not against the Lord. But there are also sins that are committed against the

Lord only. David's sin was of this last kind. Perhaps, however, you might be asking, "But what of David's sin with Bath Sheba? Did he not sin against her husband—to whom she was now prohibited—as well as against the Lord?"

According to tradition, Uriah—as was the custom with the warriors in Israel—gave his wife a bill of divorcement before he went off to battle. Thus, David did not sin against Uriah in the sense of having perfidiously robbed him of his wife. Therefore we read, "And David comforted Bath Sheba, his wife"—proof that Bath Sheba was considered David's lawful wife, destined for him since the beginning of time.

David's sin was thus an offense against the Lord alone. And of what did that offense consist? It did not lie in the fact that he had commanded Joab, his general, to send Uriah into the forefront of the battle so that he might be killed; David had a right to do so, because Uriah had called Joab "my lord Joab" while in the king's presence, which was disrespectful. Rather, the sin of David lay in the fact that he did not have Uriah killed at that point, when he had disgraced the king, but instead allowed him to be killed by the sword of the children of Ammon. For on every Ammonite sword was engraved a crooked snake that was their god. Said the Lord to David: "Thou hast imparted strength to that abomination. When the sons of Ammon had killed Uriah and many other Israelites, and the sword of Ammon prevailed, the pagan god had been strengthened by David." It can thus be seen that had Uriah granted Bath Sheba a divorce immediately, he might never have been placed in the position of insulting King David—an event that in turn led to a death sentence for Uriah.

Another source that may shed light on the issue of soulmates can be found in the writings of the Ari:

> When a new soul enters this world, mean-
> ing a soul that comes to this world for the first
> time, his soulmate accompanies him. When the
> time approaches for them to be joined in matri-
> mony, she will appear without any difficulty.
> They will instantly fall in love with each other
> and marry.

> However, should the male incur a *tikune*
> debt and require a reincarnation, his female soul
> counterpart will return with him and assist in his
> *tikune* process. This time around, however, he
> will encounter obstacles all along the way before
> he meets up again with his soulmate. Inasmuch
> as he incurred a *tikune* or debt, there are meta-
> physical cosmic forces that will make every
> attempt to prevent this soulmate marriage.

The forces described above come about as a result of one's negative actions, which incur a *tikune* debt. By living a negative lifestyle in a prior lifetime, the subject above has brought on himself a cosmic negative influence that makes his reunion with his soulmate all the more difficult. Yet he himself is the cause of his misfortune that prevents happiness with his soulmate from becoming a lover's reality. When any part of our universe departs from its balanced structure in such a way that it endangers the harmony of our cosmology, a pattern of imbalance arises. More precisely, the *tikune* law of action and reaction applies. As a result, the balance and harmony that a soul marriage provides for its participants are diminished.

When a marriage takes place in which both partners truly share in all their thoughts and actions, going forth together to accomplish a common goal that will benefit others, this indicates a true and everlasting soul marriage. Were it not a soul marriage, harmony and peace could not reign supreme.

23

Cosmic Soulmates

I trust that readers have by now come to recognize that many of our shortcomings in life, as well as many aspects of life that influence our well-being, are directly related to a predetermined *tikune* process. Those who seek enlightenment must therefore strive to make use of the many laws and principles of the metaphysical world that are at work in their own lives.

But how can we find the key that will tell us whom we should marry in order to realize a union filled with boundless joy? Astrology, or the science of cosmic influences, affects all areas of human experience, including the province of matrimony. It can have much to say, for example, about the relationship that will develop between two people who are contemplating marriage. At the same time, however, statements such as "A Leo should not marry a Cancerian" are sheer nonsense. Kabbalistic astrology neither could nor would venture to say who should marry whom.

What can be said, however, is that there are certain areas of our predetermined *tikune* in which partners are likely to find living together a strain. Conversely, there will be other areas of life to which their union may be particularly well suited. If nothing else, astrology can shed light on significant facets of one's personality, stimulating both partners to take a hard look at their true feelings before committing to marriage.

The charts reveal much about the interrelationship between potential marriage partners. Such information can give potential partners valuable insight by revealing aspects of each other's personalities that might otherwise have taken years to emerge. In particular, this book will offer advice about the selection of a timely cosmic month or day for marriage.

From a kabbalistic perspective, the cosmic influences that prevail on the day or evening of a marriage will strongly affect that union for its duration. Here again, this information should not be construed as offering rigid guidelines on what one should or should not do; it is intended only as a means of lending clarity to the situation. Ultimately, the participants must make their own decisions.

Before we can begin to fathom the influences of our cosmos, one important issue that must be explored is, "Why are the planets of the solar system, along with the sun and the moon, the only viable intelligent energy sources that soulmates should consider when they are contemplating marriage?" *The Zohar* broadens our perception of cosmic entities so that we begin to think of those entities in terms of intelligence rather than merely as energy taking the form of cosmic rays, which are essentially streams of particles.

In the kabbalistic view, humankind, like all other life forms, is part of an inseparable whole. The intelligence of celestial bodies implies that the whole has intelligence as well. Man is seen as the manifested proof of cosmic intelligence. Inasmuch as there are seven varied forms of intelligence in our universe, these seven heavenly bodies—the sun, the moon, Saturn, Jupiter, Mars, Venus, and Mercury—are the designated celestial channels through which the seven cosmic intelligence forces become manifest on earth.

A birth chart can be defined as a map of the heavens as the newborn child would see it at the moment of its birth. As has just been stated, man and the celestial bodies are part of an inseparable whole. When a particular planet rules at the time of birth, the cosmic influence of that planet provides us with a reflection of our own essence. The internal intelligence prevailing at the time of birth gives us a comprehensive picture of who we basically are.

It is therefore apparent that those who seek true soulmates must be given not only access to this information but also the means to use it, together with the spiritual understanding they will need to guarantee a soulmate marriage. The mystery of the technique alone, however, does not necessarily ensure a perfect marriage. An elevated state of consciousness, complemented by spiritual awareness, must also be achieved before a male can become worthy of his soulmate.

Virtually no changes have taken place in astrological theory since the days of Abraham. Now, as in ancient times, the planets remain the principal life forms of our universe. Their movements continue to be used to explore and elaborate on the present. From a kabbalistic perspective, each moving planet has a special relationship with a fixed sign of the Zodiac. The sun and the moon rule one sign each, and the other planets rule two signs each.

Astrology and Kabbalah both point to a unity between man and the universe. On the basis of this fundamental understanding, a record can be provided of the channels along which cosmic energy-intelligences are transmitted from the outer world to the inner nature of man. This record indicates how two partners will react to experience as it clashes all around them, as well as how they will react to each other. All of us know, as if by instinct, that the sum total of our happiness lies in the mystery of ourselves. Yet the root source of human conduct is always hidden from the eye. There is no real means of scientifically proving anything about man's inner nature. The human soul, its objectives, and its every motive and characteristic continue to elude detection.

Consequently, when the eminent medieval scholar Saadiah Gaon authored a commentary on the *Sefer Yetzirah* providing us with an in-depth view of the cosmos, the key to the mystery of cosmic energy-intelligence was at last revealed:

> This is the rule concerning the four elements: Fire and earth detest each other; fire and air love each other; fire and water simply hate each other; earth and water endear each other; earth and air abhor each other; and fire and fire feel happy with each other.

Aries (*Taleh*), Leo (*Aryeh*), and Sagittarius (*Keshet*) are masculine fire signs.

Gemini (*Teumim*), Libra (*Moznaim*), and Aquarius (*D'li*) are masculine air signs.

Cancer (*Sartan*), Scorpio, (*Akrav*), and Pisces (*Dagim*) are female water signs.

Taurus (*Shor*), Virgo (*Betulah*), and Capricorn (*G'di*) are female earth signs.

The sun has always been the most powerful of all the celestial bodies. It portrays the personality so vividly that an amazingly accurate picture can be given of the individual who was born when it was exercising its cosmic influence through a known channel of a particular sign of the zodiac.

Furthermore, states Saadiah, although one Hebrew letter created Aries and the Hebrew month of Nissan, Aries does not necessarily rule throughout Nissan. The sign of Aries makes its influence felt in the cosmos beginning in the spring and continues to exert that influence for just over 30 days. Then Taurus and Gemini follow for a period of 30 days each, completing a total of 91 days and seven and one-half hours. The summer season begins with Cancer, followed by Leo and Virgo. So it is for Libra, Scorpio, and Sagittarius beginning in the fall. Finally, Capricorn, Aquarius, and Pisces comprise the winter season.

Of course, all this does not mean that only sun signs should be taken into account. The Hebrew months, which are based on a lunar-solar system, exert a cosmic influence as well. What we are considering here, however, is the study of one's sun sign as a means of offering a glimpse of one's soulmate. And while the sun is not the only element influencing human behavior, it is surely the most important single factor in that regard.

It should be added that only a natal chart, calculated for the exact hour and minute of your birth, can yield a complete personal chart.

So just what is a sun sign? Briefly stated, it is a particular region of the Zodiac—such as Aries, Gemini, or Aquarius—in which the sun was located at the moment we drew our first breath.

Taken all together, who matches up with whom? Certainly the fire signs feel very happy with one another, as do earth and water and, in the same manner, fire and air. This compatibility is quite understandable. Life forces here on earth testify to it.

Earth requires water in its efforts to provide sustenance for the world. Air must fan a fire for the fire's continued existence. One intelligence force complements the activities of the other. The lack of either intelligence force brings about an incompleteness in the other. One needs and requires the other. There is no ego involved; both elements recognize their inadequacy. This is a true soulmate.

When one partner in a marriage seems to manage alone, we know that the union is not one of soulmates. If mutual interest in spiritual or other matters that pertain to the welfare of others does not exist between partners, a soul marriage is out of the question.

At this point, however, it is important that mention be made of the reincarnation principle as it affects marriages outside the framework of soulmates. The female half of any soulmate is not required to return to assist her male counterpart. Females are not required to be reincarnated. "The cleansing of the soul in purgatory is sufficient for females," states the Ari. In cases where the male must be reincarnated to fulfill the *tikune* process, the female counterpart of this soul may elect to stay where all souls, having no further debt to pay, remain. So those of you who are not married to your soulmate need not be disappointed. Your present time around fits into the overall program of the *tikune* process.

To return to our subject of soulmates, the ground rules as laid down by Saadiah Gaon are exceptionally clear. Persons with an Arian influence are enthusiastic and generous and have an instant smile. At the same time, the Arian is conscious only of himself. Arians may be quick-tempered— they are no diplomats—and are at their worst completely absorbed with themselves. Their needs come first. An Arian may be so intent on looking after himself that he might forget to consider even his closest friends.

Superficially speaking, these are accurate descriptions of a strong Arian character. Nevertheless, the contradictions are equally visible. If the true Arian is so generous, for example, why do we include selfishness among his more prominent traits? The answer to this and many other obvious contradictions are more fully described in my book on astrology. What we are concerned with here, however, is not so much the "why" of things. The purpose of this chapter is to provide the reader with enough material and information to determine if their existing or contemplated marriage is indeed one that involves soulmates.

Consequently, the knowledge furnished by Saadiah Gaon is intended to provide a cosmic, internal printout for people concerned with the matter of soulmates.

The water signs, according to Saadiah, do not interact well with Leo, Aries, or Sagittarius. Water and fire do not go well together. In fact, according to *The Zohar*, the internal intelligence of water, which is positive by nature, is intent on extinguishing all forms of internal intelligence ruled by fire. Fire is negative in its essence. Correspondingly, the internal intelligence of fire is determined to prevail over water and to sear and dry it up.

Observable water and fire are merely the physical manifestations and expressions of the internal intelligences to which we have referred. Once the materialization disappears, the internal energy-intelligence is no longer a viable force. Without its vessel, water, the internal intelligence of positivity returns to its potential state of inactivity. In the absence of the physical expression of the flame, the negative internal intelligence reverts to its original motionless state. To be sure, no form of internal intelligence disappears. Instead, what disappears is the vessel or element that makes possible the physical expression of these extraterrestrial (nonphysical) intelligences. If the water no longer exists, then its internal energy force (intelligence) can no longer express itself. It lies dormant until such time as the physical vessel or channel is again permitted to surface.

This is the essence of the continuous conflict between, say, a Leonine and a Scorpion. The internal intelligences of these two signs conflict with one another. Consequently, one or the other must ultimately yield lest all hell break loose. In the final analysis, while each may learn to live with the other, these signs seldom if ever complement or fire the enthusiasm of their mate. This is not the definition of a soulmate. There is nothing really complicated or difficult about Leo. He is king—and make no mistake about it. I know, as I myself am a Leo. Leos need the opportunity to express their natural and considerable potential. The water signs are simply do not meet the task of fanning the flames.

However, were the Cancerian, Scorpion, and Piscean teamed up with the earth signs, each partner would have a better chance of expressing their individual internal intelligence energies. Water was created for the express purpose of assisting mother earth in her flourishing endeavor to provide sustenance to the world.

The land provides the internal intelligence of water, the element of sharing, with the opportunity to express itself. One force complements the other. This could indeed point to a union of true soulmates.

But try uniting a Libran with a Taurean, and what do you find? The internal intelligence of a Libran is the character of the central column. As such, Librans demonstrate the ability to mediate between others and to restore harmony. They are always in the middle, moving from one opposing side to the other—restless, if you will. In their attempt to balance the scales, Librans must always traverse the long road of the balancing process itself. First one side is higher, and then the other. This process continues until perfect balance is attained.

A Taurean embraces and envelops the intelligence of earth. The fabric of this intelligence is its desire to be the recipient of things that go on all around it. It loves to be part of the landscape, a permanent fixture abhorring movement— the epitome of the Desire to Receive. But put a Taurean together with a Libran and you have the makings of a windstorm. The Taurean will not be rushed or moved as the Libran partner would have it. The intelligence of possessiveness, rather than that of reaching out, is the decisive energy factor that determines the character of a Taurean. The Libran will have no part of this. Life with a Taurean is too dull and boring. Permit the Libran to fan the fire of a Leo, however, and see them shine and smile.

It is for this very reason that fire signs are not real soulmates of earthborn intelligence forces. The Leonine is magnanimous, expansive, and even intrusive. Taureans would rather be taking care of their immediate needs. The bull seldom rushes forward to take the initiative; he simply wants to be left alone. His internal intelligence force is like mother earth, or perhaps like the rock of Gibraltar—solid, steady, immovable, and so persevering that it will not budge an inch. A Taurean simply could not dance to the same tune as the Leonine.

If you think the Aquarian could fare any better with the Taurean, then you have another guess coming. If there is anyone that can really unnerve the Taurean, it's the Aquarian. While friendly, Aquarians often prefer to remain detached. They are extremely faithful and loyal but are at the same time thoroughly unpredictable. Personal independence is of great importance to them, even to the point of temporarily rejecting intimate and close friends and relatives. People born under this air sign can really toss up a tempestuous wind with their fellow Taureans.

Saadiah Gaon seems to have given us ample information with which to help us choose our life partner. This is not to say, however, that those who do not fit the appropriate description should hurry off to the nearest divorce agency. To the contrary, the information given herein should be regarded only as a tool with which to understand the positive and negative aspects of one's relationship. They may be there for the sole purpose of your spiritual growth.

24

THE MARRIAGE EXERCISE

According to kabbalistic teachings, the dissolution of a marriage is not prohibited but at the same time should never be taken lightly. The Bible allows couples to divorce if they find it beyond their power to live together. In this way, they can go their separate ways to forge new and better unions rather than remain bound to a lifetime of unhappiness. But before a divorce can take place, an effort toward peacemaking must first be made. The task of counseling and striving to adjust the grievances of the parties involved should be entrusted to a spiritually enlightened person, and only when even that person's efforts have failed can a divorce proceed.

To be sure, this system worked well over the centuries. The Bible's central purpose—which is the preservation of marriage—was largely achieved. Today, however, it is not unusual to find relationships in which no attempt at compromise or reconciliation is made. Good will, perseverance, and adaptability are set aside. The Bible's intention is not just defeated, but ignored.

It goes without saying that no couple has identical tastes or habits. When two people live together in the intimate setting of marriage, differences in taste, habit, and outlook are certain to emerge. Often this reaps disastrous results both for the couple and for those who live with and around them. Sadly, however, these differences are often trivial and of little consequence in and of themselves.

Divorce that is based solely on superficial disagreements can only be the result of lost spirituality. When a couple agrees on spiritual matters, other differences automatically fade in significance. There can be no bitterness or dissension between a husband and wife who share each other's ideals.

Physical and material aspects of marriage have their place, but spiritual principles must come first. The spiritual presence in family life is what hallows the union of man and wife. This ensures that their children will be blessed with purity as well as with health. A soul conceived in the holiness of wedlock will, at the moment of conception, enter into the fullness of life endowed with the purity that will stand as the guarantee of his character.

It requires little study of society, with its hatreds, wars, and crimes, to recognize souls conceived under other circumstances. *The Zohar* teaches that the thoughts of a man and woman during sexual intercourse determine what sort of soul will occupy the body of their child. When the thoughts and feelings of a married couple are as they should be, the physical and sexual expression of marriage may then follow as a sanctified action—and the positive character of the children will be assured.

Of necessity, ideas of modesty and morality are inherent in our attitude toward marriage. Without them, marriage is little more than the cohabitation of two individuals who may fear and hate each other in the depths of their hearts with an intensity that not even they can fathom. Happy is the man whose wife bestows love and faith on the union and who is to him mother, sister, wife, and friend, sharing all his burdens and caring and sustaining the household, even in times of adversity, with love and peace. But if a man cannot understand his own soul and the soul of the woman he loves, and if that love is not based on knowledge of reincarnation and deeper understanding, there is no foundation on which marriage can be built.

In view of all the pain and pitfalls that inevitably attend even the best of marriages, it seems remarkable that anyone would choose to get married at all. Yet in the United States at least, the institution of marriage is finding favor as never before. There is within the human heart an innate intuition to seek a spouse.

Kabbalistic law states that every man has a duty to marry in order to procreate children. This is made clear in *The Bible*: ". . . and the Almighty blessed them and said unto them, 'be fruitful and multiply and replenish earth!' " From Genesis onward, the obligation of motherhood has been bestowed upon women, and that obligation is consistent throughout all sacred literature. It is the primary duty for which a woman was formed. Thus, when Adam named his partner, he called her Hava (Eve) because she was the mother of Hal (all the living). According to *The Zohar*, names always signify the major functions in creation of those who bear them. Hence Eve's name contains within it the function for which she was created.

The Bible consistently emphasizes the importance of procreation. Sarah's unhappiness at being barren gives way to happiness when Isaac is born to her. Rebecca, in preparing for marriage, receives the blessing that she will have children. Rachel voices pure misery when she says to Jacob, "Give me children or else I will die." David sings, "Thy wife shall be as fruitful as a fruitful vine." With such an underpinning, marriage has always been considered a divinely ordained institution in which the duty of procreation may be fulfilled.

There is always more to *The Bible* than first meets the eye. Essentially, it is written in a code to which Kabbalah is the key. As *The Zohar* puts it, "Those who consider the stories of the Torah to indicate merely a story are foolish and uninformed, for if that were the case, then the supernal Torah, which is full of holiness and truth, could have been written by anyone who was qualified to write beautiful stories."

The Bible is filled with stories of lust and perversion, but because it is more than just a television script, these accounts must be read and understood at a far deeper level than is generally accepted. It is incumbent upon us to understand the inner mystical meaning of *The Bible* in connection with marriage and procreation. Biblical precepts that guard the purity of marriage are a critical factor in creating a strong relationship between husband and wife, and in ensuring that children born of such a union will bear the imprint of that relationship throughout their lives. We cannot, however, ignore the instability and lack of devotion that mar most modern marriages. We must come to grips with the reality of today—a reality that has made the noble words of our sages ring empty and hollow. If we are to return to the beautiful aspects of marriage, a thorough understanding of reincarnation is necessary.

25

REINCARNATION AND
GIVEN NAMES

A key factor in achieving control of our lives lies in the choice of a given name or last names are of no importance; they are worn and discarded like so many suits of clothes in the course of many incarnations. The given name, however, is crucial and must be chosen to be congruent with the individual soul. Parents should always name their children after relatives or loved ones who were giving people, and with whom they felt a soul affinity. Kabbalistically, they really have no choice beyond selecting the name the child brings into the world from past incarnations. They may think they have chosen, but in reality, they have not.

Naming a child after someone other than a loved one sets that child at odds with his own identity, especially if the namesake has died in a particularly violent or bizarre manner. The name can burden the child with a remnant of the *tikune* that was being working out at the time of death.

Frequently, a parent will come to me with a problem involving a son or a daughter. Inevitably, my first question is, "For whom was the child named?" In virtually every case, the problem will be less with the child than with the namesake whose particular vices the child is reflecting.

At various times, biblical names have been fashionable. People have named their children Joshua, Adam, or even Enoch. Then, inexplicably, the popularity of biblical names yields to more secular choices. The kabbalistic explanation is that biblical names prevail in periods of revelation and enlightenment, whereas retreat from such names takes place as darkness descends over the human spirit. More than any other names, those selected from *The Bible* are constructed from Hebrew letters, which are vehicles of energy transfer. The Bible includes a specific verse for each name, and whoever meditates on their own verse will find themselves at the threshold of the time tunnel that leads back to memory of previous incarnations. There, body and circumstances were different, but the name was unchanged.

So powerful is the influence of a name, and so powerful is the negativity surrounding the wrong name, that a kabbalistic answer for great physical or spiritual illness frequently lies in a name change. This can steer the individual back to connection with his true identity. Like any technique, this is not foolproof, but virtually every case of conflict within an individual personality can be traced to an improperly assigned name.

A young man enrolled in one of my reincarnation classes, for example, had a son who had been born with a birth defect. The child had no muscular support in the right side of his neck, and as a result, his head leaned to the right.

In search of a cause for this affliction, we discussed the father's family background. The young man revealed that his sister had been murdered before the birth of the afflicted child. The murder weapon was a gun, and the fatal bullet had ripped through the right side of his sister's neck. Although the child in question was a boy, his given name was similar to that of his father's sister. Obviously, the child was the reincarnation of that woman. The child's health problem could have been prevented had the parents been able to understand and apply the principles of reincarnation at the time the child was conceived. As this example shows, an understanding of reincarnation takes us to the level of consciousness where the causes of visible effects lie buried. To approach such problems without making that journey is like trying to fight crabgrass with a lawnmower.

Through knowledge of reincarnation, an individual can probe not only into the immediate causes of problems, but into the causes of those causes as well. The extent to which a person uses such knowledge, of course, is entirely a matter of choice. Some may be content to gain one small glimmer of illumination while others aim at nothing less than final liberation from the wheel of reincarnation itself. But for all who achieve it, the ability to recollect former existences means freedom from materialist obsessions and a greater appreciation for spirituality in mind and soul. Knowledge of reincarnation and of kabbalistic meditation techniques, therefore, can have a very practical impact on how we live our lives.

A person who is in financial distress, for example, can gain insight into his problems—and even find their solution—by reexperiencing more pleasurable and affluent periods in prior lifetimes. The depressed can find hope, the grieving solace, and the imprisoned freedom. The teachings of Kabbalah include a wealth of meditative techniques with which to transcend the limits of a present incarnation. A full discussion of meditation could fill many books, so for now I will only urge readers to begin exploring kabbalistic meditation as soon as possible.

26

GLOBAL INCARNATION

Why do some nations become ever wealthier while others stagnate financially to the point of economic disaster? Why have certain parts of the world experienced incredible scientific development while others have actually gone in the opposite direction?

These are some of the most puzzling and difficult questions faced by contemporary historians. The complexity of today's human interactions, on an individual as well as an international scale, makes it almost impossible to precisely identify reasons for economic progress or regress. It has been suggested that a society that is intolerant of criticism and suppresses dissent may be vulnerable to stagnation. In contrast, a society permitting dissent and tolerance of new ideas will benefit from continuous innovation. But these explanations only circumvent the basic principle of cause and effect. The fallacy in this type of reasoning lies in the fact that cause and effect have not been distinguished. Which comes first, the chicken or the egg? Tolerance or lack of tolerance may be the result of a progressive society rather than the cause of it.

We seem to know little concerning primal cause. This is why so much has been written on the topic of societal progress, with very few definitive answers. I have stressed the need for a complete reorientation of our analytical process. The kabbalistic view of our universe holds great promise for revealing a single coherent picture of reality. It proposes that, when seeking the true causes of events, we must take the whole universe into account—even down to the quantum level. Baffling as it may seem, quantum theory points to faster-than-light connections in which cosmic intelligences may provide measuring devices and techniques by which science will correlate and connect states of spatially separated entities. In other words, our universe need not remain an eternal mystery.

How has progress of this kind taken place in the past? Now and then, scientists have stumbled across facts that seem to solve one of the great mysteries of civilization. Such unexpected discoveries are usually rare and far between. When they do occur, however, they generally prove less revolutionary than was first believed. Usually they fail once again to explain those rudimentary, fundamental evolutionary precepts that have hardly changed at all throughout history.

With all the changes that science has wrought, how much real change has taken place? War, hate, envy, anger, and other forms of human chaos seem little affected by the environmental changes constantly taking place all around us.

The real question is, what is this Force that can exert such never-ending control over the psyche of man, and yet at the same time permit extraordinary outbursts of innovations and breakthroughs? What is the catalyst behind the remarkable outpouring of new technology in the past few years? What is the power that allows for so much change while at the same time leaving so much unchanged, seemingly forever?

The startling revelation that creatures are different because of different varieties of spiritual energy, infused by the Force, accounts in great measure for the psychic differences among human beings—and also for the differences among nations and their natural resources. The basic building blocks for both individual and national identities come from the same cosmic Force, which becomes manifest in seven orbiting structures, the seven planets.

In connection with this, the idea that the Force radiates energy through the sun within the solar system is not new. Why are planetary probes or artificial satellites equipped with solar energy systems? From a kabbalistic perspective, we merely reflect inward, just as a physicist probes inward toward the elusive world of subatomic phenomena. Rather than taking the sun as the primal force of energy, *The Zohar* states that all manifested forms of energy are merely the result of natural, intelligent cosmic emissions that ultimately become clothed in orbital channels. These cosmic beacons all originate in the Force and become differentiated as they pass through terrestrial orbital channels. Consequently, it comes as no surprise when these cosmic intelligences are detected and seen as messengers from the Force, seeding earth with complex organic intelligent forms.

These encapsulated, intelligent coded messages, known as Sfirot, are a kind of metaphysical DNA. They are the primal forces that account for our solar system as well as for earth's variety of nations, cultures, and environments. Under their influence, the earth has produced a network of societies that provide the cultural birthright of every race, with its specific science, intelligence, art, and history. One day, some of humankind's most talented minds might decode these interstellar messages and discover the intelligent civilizations of outer space—civilizations that have long been known by the kabbalists. In a word, these extraterrestrial messages are the complex forms of Sfirot that encapsulate the Force.

As *The Zohar* explains, the seven forms of intelligence that emanate from the seven Sfirot are directly responsible for all manifestation throughout the universe. Advanced extraterrestrial noncorporeal beings living in a solar system similar to ours direct the orbiting structures of our own universe. They are also responsible for the varying degrees of the Force that are present in different areas of our planet.

All life dances to the music of astral influences. Unseen extraterrestrial forces affect earthly affairs and determine the cycles of human affairs. If the scientific community could accept the hypothesis that earthly activity is subject to cosmic influence—as *The Zohar* clearly states—vast new frontiers of knowledge would be opened. Natural phenomena throughout creation would be seen to depend on an infinitely powerful cosmic force.

This force has an intelligence that expresses itself in numberless ways. It can be compared to the human soul, which makes every individual different from every other.

The soul is responsible for a person's creativity, for free will, and for emotions such as love, hate, fear, and courage. The seven nonmaterial entities cause the individual diversity of the universe and earth. The various regions of the earth, therefore, are directly related to the aspect of cosmic intelligence that resides in a particular area.

This intelligence force affects its inhabitants in the same way a programmer directs a computer or a pilot maneuvers an airplane. Specific levels of intelligence are responsible for specific geographical locations. An inhabitant of Germany, for example, is not under the same cosmic influence as someone in Russia or Mexico. Traits and customs that characterize one nation cannot and are not similar to those of any other. These differences are the direct result of each nation's peculiar cosmic influence.

Does this revelation mean that all people of one nation behave alike? Of course not! People remain individuals. Then how do we reconcile the establishment of clearly defined national characteristics due particular cosmic energies with the ability of every person to maintain unique traits and behaviors?

There is also another mystery I would like to explore, and that is the conflict between continuous change and mankind's stubborn insistence on clinging to well-defined modes of behavior. The very process of change that is evident everywhere also makes us wonder how life forms continue unchanged for so long. All life forms, including human beings, desire the very same things that their ancestors desired. Startling technological breakthroughs have had very little effect on human thought and emotion.

Is our frame of mind really different from that of the people of the Middle Ages? Have human needs really changed down through the centuries? Fundamentally, the answer is no. But should we, then, regard this lack of change as an evolutionary failure?

No mystery in the long history of our universe is as startling as the resistance to change in the behavior of its inhabitants. Our understanding of this is so undeveloped that we should not marvel at our continued insistence on destroying each other. If we must marvel, let it be at our own inability to unlock the secrets of human behavioral patterns. Fundamental evolutionary precepts have hardly changed throughout history. Consequently, it is truly exciting and even refreshing when we come across information that radically alters and expands our perspective. Therefore, let us turn again to *The Zohar* and its revolutionary insights on what is taking place in our lives at this pivotal moment in history. Specifically, let us recognize that neither reincarnation nor "belief in" reincarnation is a thing of the past. Indeed, as Rav Isaac Luria tells us, in our present Aquarian Age the souls of the Exodus generation shall again become incarnated.

But if the story of our universe is really a story of returning souls, what accounts for the fundamental lack of change in human nature and action?

To answer this, it is crucial to know that we have all been here before. When considering human behavioral patterns, therefore, we are essentially seeing aspects of ourselves as we were in former lifetimes. Life for most of us is virtually a rerun of some task we attempted earlier but failed to successfully complete. This is exactly the reason humanity remains in an unalterable state of mind. Why does mankind still maintain primal characteristics and cling to well-defined modes of existence? It is because man in the 21st century is a motion picture that has been run over and over again.

What Kabbalah teaches, and what I am suggesting here, is that the *tikune* process largely dictates modern man's emotional and intellectual patterns and processes. When we really grasp this fact, we gain a completely different view of human problems and complexities.

Environmental influences do not promote behavioral or physical differences among people. The returning souls leave us with our passions and petty hatreds. Rebellion against authority and abandonment of religion are traits that have shown their faces before on the stage of history. These deep-seated, innate tendencies transcend the unique cosmic influences on a section of our globe. This, then, accounts for why some nations get richer while others stagnate to the point of economic disaster. Why some societies progress and others do not can be seen as a relationship between the specific location on earth and its connection to the cosmic force.

The astral forces are most closely aligned with the physical, external characteristics that appear across the globe. They determine the natural resources that appear in one place and not in another. They govern physical qualities that make up the habitats of souls who, for reasons of the *tikune* process, locate in one particular section over another. These distinct characteristics define the soul's physical expression, and hence the area of pursuit in the *tikune* process.

Consequently, matters that relate to the exterior culture of any nation depend on the particular cosmic force governing that area. The influence of cold, rational scientific materialism in an area will depend on the intensity of the Desire to Receive of a specific astral influence generating these cosmic forces. Scientific development or the lack thereof always depends on the Desire to Receive. A wealthy and flourishing nation is nothing other than its desire to receive great power. Why does a nation retain a pattern of high technology, if not for the purpose of achieving ultimate domination and supremacy in the world?

It is precisely here that the distinction between global cosmic influence and man's free will and his innate love of sharing are most keenly felt. Criminals against humanity were placed within the particular frame of reference of cosmic negativity that prevailed over Germany. These reincarnated individuals were returning according to their earlier failure in the *tikune* process. They were now faced with the same challenge of either exercising free will and thwarting the cosmic force of extreme negativity or succumbing to its influence.

We might ask: Is this really fair? The answer lies precisely in the purpose for creation at its very inception, which is the removal of Bread of Shame. These negative frames of reference provide man with an opportunity to exercise free will and thus achieve the removal of Bread of Shame. Obviously, if these negative cosmic forces did not exist, man would simply conform to a preprogrammed form of intelligence that would dictate the sharing philosophy, leaving little room for our destructive passions, hatreds, and other traits that distinguish us from computers. While on the one hand cosmic negativity aroused and triggered heinous behavior in Nazi Germany, this influence, as powerful as it was, could have and should have been controlled by the individuals who were subject to it. This is the choice and obligation that free will imposes on us.

Jerusalem is the energy center of Israel, and Israel is the energy center of the world. This has always been true. All nations of the world—past, present, and future—become powerful only on account of Israel. Egypt, for instance, did not rule over the whole world until the people of Israel settled there. This also holds true of Babylon (586 B.C.E.), Greece (200 B.C.E.), and Rome (60 B.C.E.). Before that, all these nations were utterly insignificant and contemptible. Their greatness was due entirely to the people of Israel.

This is what *The Zohar* teaches, and the truth of its teaching becomes strikingly clear if we consider the fate of the land of Israel in relation to the history of other nations. We find the Persian empire of Cyrus reaching its peak at a time when Jews were living in exile in that country. A similar phenomenon occurs in the case of the Babylonian, Greek, and Roman empires and, more recently, the Ottoman Empire. The most recent example of this extraordinary pattern is the British Empire. In each case, the country in question reached the peak of its international influence at the time when it ruled over the people and especially the Land of Israel, and measured its decline from the time when it lost possession of that land.

When patterns begin forming, we should consider the metaphysical forces behind them. *The Zohar* reveals the internal cosmic forces that shape the history of our universe. Regarding *The Zohar*'s description of Israel, one cannot but notice the interconnectedness between former world powers and Israel's intrinsic energy center. This is precisely the reason nations have sought to capture its energy resources. However, cautions *The Zohar*, the mysterious cosmic powerhouse of that land can also bring destruction to those who lack the proper bond of cosmic connection.

Here we are given yet another example of earth's atmospheric influence over humankind's destiny. Providing an incarnated soul with an environment that meets the specifications of the *tikune* process will result in some souls appearing in a particular part of the globe so as to fulfill their tikune. Consequently, when we raised the question of why things happen as they do in one area and not another, we see that the people making history were destined to return where they did, exerting astral influences on earth as an integral element of reincarnation.

27

ATLANTIS

C ivilizations are born, make their imprint on history, and eventually die. This process will continue until the final curtain on the Age of Aquarius comes down. ·

The story of the island of Atlantis is narrated in Plato's dialogues. Atlantis ruled Africa as far as the border of Egypt, and Europe to Tuscany on the Apennine peninsula. But suddenly the island was destroyed by an earthquake and other natural disturbances. It sank into the ocean and vanished forever.

According to Plato, the inhabitants of this island had reached a highly sophisticated level of development, both materially and spiritually. Their cosmic consciousness was such that they had achieved full control of energy fields and their environment. But there were some among them who attempted to use this enormous power to enslave others. A struggle then developed, resulting in the eventual destruction of their land.

The earthquakes were a direct result of this human conflict. It was the clash between good and evil that wrought this "natural" disaster. The survivors who managed to reach other lands took an oath that their knowledge would never again be revealed to the world. The secrets of cosmic and solar energy would remain with the select few. Aspirants would have to demonstrate the ability to correctly make use of this secret knowledge long before any teaching would become available. Then and only then, when the student was ready, would the master appear. And the selected students received knowledge only to the extent that they were prepared to use it "not for themselves alone."

While many thought that the tale of Atlantis was a figment of Plato's imagination, even today the legend refuses to die. Poets and novelists have exploited the tale freely. Men of science have been more cautious.

In the latter part of the 19th century, expeditions searched the Atlantic Ocean for remnants of Atlantis. Societies were created for the purpose of investigating the phenomenon of the sunken island. While there has been much speculation as to its whereabouts, the research and discussions concerning the cultural and scientific achievements seem to be far more interesting.

Were there really civilizations equal to or more advanced in information sciences than our own? We consider our own era to be the most enlightened and sophisticated in all of history, and the story of Atlantis is regarded as a myth. To some extent, this belief results from the fact that a great deal of information about the past has been lost.

The great libraries of the ancient world, for example, seem to have vanished into thin air. Even by our own standards, the vastness of the library of Alexandria is incredible. Created in 330 B.C. in honor of Alexander the Great, the city of Alexandria held an enormous library containing about 700,000 rare books. All this was destroyed when Julius Caesar burned the great library to the ground, forever separating mankind from this treasure of priceless information. Similarly, the city of Carthage, in North Africa, saw its great library of more than half a million volumes destroyed by the Roman Legions in 146 B.C.

Although much of man's ancient intellectual heritage seems to have been permanently lost, *The Bible* persists as a source of historical knowledge. Yet *The Bible* is rarely given credit as an accurate expression of the human past. In my opinion, this neglect is attributable to *The Bible's* astonishing detail and accuracy, down to every single letter and punctuation. The Bible's authenticity is too precise and sharply focused for conventional historians and scientific investigators. This, of course, is the reason we must finally give appropriate attention to *The Bible* as a historical record of what happened, why it happened, and when it happened.

There are no episodes in *The Bible* that appeal more strongly to the human imagination than those of the Great Flood and the generation of the tower of Babel. Returning to our question as to whether former civilizations were advanced in information sciences, let us look at a biblical passage concerning the Tower of Babel:

And the whole earth was of one language [Hebrew] and of one speech. And it came to pass, as they journeyed eastward [miqedem], that they found a plain in the land of Shinar, and they dwelt there.

The Zohar explains that the word miqedem means "away from the source of the world." Regarding the phrase "that they found," we might have expected "that they saw." But the word found indicates that they discovered remnants of the secret wisdom that had been left by the generation of the Flood, and with that they made an attempt to locate the source. *The Zohar* continues:

Note what is written [in *The Bible*]. "Behold they are one people and they have all one language. Being of one mind, of one will, and speaking one language, nothing will be withheld from them, which they purpose to do . . . The supernal judgment was powerless against them." Rav Jose said: From here we learn that quarrelsome people soon come to grief, for we see here that as long as the peoples of the world lived in harmony, being of one mind and one will, although they rebelled against the source, the supernal judgment could not touch them, but as soon as they were divided, "the Lord scattered them abroad."

The events of the Great Flood and the Tower of Babel brought overwhelming destruction to the entire world. That of the Flood was most devastating. Water covered the land and annihilated the inhabitants of earth, erasing every memory of what had happened up to that time. And the secret wisdom mentioned in *The Zohar*, which was the awesome power of former civilizations, disappeared under the water.

The civilization of the Babel era bore witness to real science born in the remotest periods of antiquity. Advanced civilizations, vastly different and in some cases greater than our own, existed in past history, as recorded in *The Bible*. The Babel civilization was fragmented by God's confounding its language, but it was reestablished with the demise of the Middle Kingdom of Egypt and the great Exodus. It reached its summit during the period of the First and Second Temples. The destruction of the Second Temple brought with it the disappearance of this awesome power. It would not appear again until the Age of Aquarius.

While modern historians reject the idea that ancient man possessed advanced knowledge, there is much evidence to indicate that great technological proficiency did exist during ancient times. How, then, did ancient man acquire this knowledge? *The Zohar* explains that God did indeed send down a book to Adam from which Adam became acquainted with the supernal wisdom of the Light. This book was brought down to Adam by the master of mysteries, the Angel Raziel. The book later came into the hands of the "sons of the Lord"—that is, the wise souls of their generation. Whoever was privileged to peruse it acquired the wisdom of the Light and its awesome power.

Three angels always accompanied and kept watch over
the book so as to prevent its falling into improper hands.
When Adam was expelled from the Garden of Eden, he tried
to keep the book, but it flew out of his hands. Weeping, he
prayed to the Lord for its return. It was given back to him in
order that the wisdom would not be forgotten, and that
mankind might strive to obtain knowledge of The Creator
by understanding the Light. Happy are those people of exalted spiritual piety to whom the wisdom has been revealed, and
by whom it will never be forgotten. As *The Bible* states: "The
secret of the Lord is with them."

This divinely given book was the fount from which
spiritual man could draw from to fill his thirst for knowledge,
wisdom, and power. Through the Golden Age of Rav
Shimon bar Yohai, sages possessed knowledge of a kind modern science can hardly even imagine.

Did Atlantis ever exist as a physical location? And if
not, where did the idea of Atlantis originate? Historians have
been of the opinion that the tale of Atlantis was an illusion of
Plato. Yet Plato himself had no access to any literary works
that might have described what Atlantis actually looked like.
By Plato's time, much knowledge of previous civilizations
had perished. Plato could only record a story that was said to
have been heard by the Greek ruler known as Solon, during
a visit to the high priests of Egypt:

> The ocean that was there at that time was
> navigable. For in the front of its mouth [we
> might understand this to mean Gibraltar] which
> you Greeks call the Pillars of Heracles, there lay

an island which was larger than Lybia and Asia together. It was possible for the travelers of that time to cross from it to other islands, and from the islands onward to the whole of the continent over against them which encompasses that ocean. Beyond is a real ocean, and the land surrounding it may be considered a continent. In this Island of Atlantis existed a confederation of kings of great and marvelous power, which held sway over the entire island and many other lands.

The priest told Solon that one day this mighty kingdom sank forever into the ocean. But what of its inhabitants? Did they drown, or did their advanced information remain alive? Although Atlantis is generally quite unwilling to reveal its secrets, I will attempt to tell you something of its existence and the nature of the people who inhabited it.

Whenever The Creator has allowed the deep mysteries of wisdom to be brought down into the world, mankind has become corrupt. God gave supernal wisdom to Adam, but Adam used this wisdom to familiarize and attach himself to the evil inclination, and the fountains of wisdom were closed to him. After Adam repented, some of the wisdom was again revealed to him. The civilization of Babel, by virtue of this wisdom, provoked the Lord and built a tower. They did various kinds of mischief until they were scattered over the face of the earth.

Noah received the wisdom, but afterward "he drank of the wine and was drunken and uncovered." The wisdom was then given to Abraham, who, by means of it, served the Almighty. But then his son Ishmael provoked the Lord. Isaac received the wisdom, but his son Esau also provoked the Lord. As for Jacob, the wisdom was not complete inasmuch as he married two sisters. The Creator also gave the wisdom to Moses, of whom it is written: "He is trusted in all my house."

Now, in the Age of Aquarius, The Creator will cause the wisdom to be disseminated throughout the world. All the peoples of the world will use it for worthwhile purposes, as it is written: "And I will set my spirit within you." This is in contrast with the generations of old, who used wisdom for the ruin and exploitation of the world.

While *The Zohar* points to the reappearance of the wisdom, we must ask by what method or teaching "all peoples of the world" will acquire it. Regarding this, *The Zohar* describes an incident in which Rav Jose and Rav Judah entered a cavern. At the far end, they found a book hidden in the cleft of a rock. Rav Jose brought it out and caught sight of 72 tracings of letters that had been given to Adam. The two men began to examine the book, and when they had studied only two or three of the letters, they found themselves contemplating the essence of supernal wisdom. But suddenly a flame struck their hands, and the book vanished from them.

When they described this event to Rav Shimon, he replied, "At this time, God does not desire so much to be revealed. But when the Age of Aquarius draws near, even little children will discover the secrets of the wisdom. At that time it will be revealed to all, as it is written, 'For then I will turn to the peoples a pure language!' "

So are we now ready to discover the wisdom and to reconnect with the Light? The answer is yes—but what became of the people who possessed this awesome power in ancient times? Where did the inhabitants of Atlantis disappear to? Why is there seemingly no trace of them anywhere in history?

Perhaps we might ask why we are so interested in Atlantis in the first place. After all, we do not seem to be so preoccupied with details of our own grandfathers and their grandfathers before them. The answer may lie in our instinctive interest in life beyond the world as we experience it every day. Throughout the ages, humankind has speculated about life on other worlds. Unfortunately or otherwise, these other worlds in our own planetary system seem barren. A much broader question, however, is whether there could be planets around other stars elsewhere in the universe.

Throughout history, there has been much speculation on the origin or purpose of the planets. No one knows which—if any—of the current theories are correct. Of greatest interest, however, is the possibility of the existence of life beyond what we see on earth. As scientists probe for evidence of extraterrestrial life forms, many are becoming increasingly outspoken about the possibility of their existence. In fact, it is no longer a question of whether there could be "somebody out there." The problem is where—and how to establish the first interplanetary dialogue.

Astrophysicists are encouraged in their probe for life in outer space by new discoveries. The presence of a great number of complicated organic molecules in the universe voids earlier theories that such life forms could not exist in space. It might appear to us that the cosmos contains a great number of unexpected and unpredictable entities.

But from a kabbalistic viewpoint, the existence of complex molecules alone would not signal the presence of other populated worlds. Intelligence sufficient to control the universe with the awesome power and wisdom of the Light requires a physical form such as ours here on earth.

One of the most remarkable accounts of other life forms I have ever read appears in *The Zohar*. This description could very well become the basis for future research:

> Rav Nehorai the Elder once went on a sea voyage. The ship was wrecked in a storm and all in it were drowned. He, however, by some miracle, went down to the bottom of the sea and found an inhabited land where he saw strange human beings of diminutive size; they were reciting prayers, but he could not tell what they said. By another miracle he then came up again. He said: "Blessed are the righteous who study the Torah and know the most profound mysteries. Woe to those who dispute with them and do not accept their word." From that day on whenever he came into the house of study and heard the Torah being expounded, he would weep. When they asked him why he wept, he would say, "Because I was skeptical about the words of the Ravs. I did not believe the existence of seven lands with inhabitants different than ourselves. Now I fear for the judgment of the other world."

By no means has *The Zohar* yielded up all
its mysteries. Even if we put aside the profound
question of travel deep into the sea to discover
an existing civilization, many questions
remain—whose answers will surely raise more
questions. As a first step, let us examine a statement by Rav Nehorai commenting on the Age of
Aquarius:

> In the generation of the Age of Aquarius,
> young men will insult the aged; old men will rise
> in the presence of the young; daughters will rise
> against their mothers and daughters-in-law
> against their mothers-in-law. The face of the
> generation shall be as the face of a dog, and a son
> will not be abashed in the presence of his father.

This is a gloomy description for the epitome of human
intellectual achievement. How can we reconcile this picture
with the concept of the Age of Aquarius as an era of supreme
enlightenment?

The Zohar answers this question through Rav Shimon,
who wept and said, "Woe unto him who meets with that
period (the Age of Aquarius), for the revelation of the enormous cosmic light of energy shall be an agonizing torment
for those not prepared to deal with it. Praiseworthy, however,
are those who shall merit the joy-giving light of the King."

For those ill prepared to meet the Age of Aquarius, the
challenge of an age of enlightenment will mean pain and distress, the likes of which the world had never experienced.

Rav Nehorai's contact with an advanced civilization moved him to tears. He realized that this civilization had suffered the fate of all those who were ill prepared to handle the profound wisdom. Here were the remnants of the peoples of the Tower of Babel—a living testimonial to what can happen to an advanced culture when the spiritual ideals of the Light and the eternal wisdom are misused.

The destruction of Atlantis as described by Plato was the inevitable result of mistreating and abusing the eternal wisdom. Adam, the peoples of the Great Flood, and the civilization of Atlantis—referred to in *The Bible* as the Tower of Babel civilization—caused Rav Nehorai to weep: "Woe unto those who are ill-prepared."

The race is now on to prepare ourselves as this wisdom reappears in the world. As we recall what had happened in the past, let us also recall the words of King David: "The Lord is our refuge and strength, a very present help in trouble. Therefore we will not fear, though the earth does change and the mountains be moved into the heart of the seas."

2 8

TELEPORTATION

Everything in the universe is energy. What we observe are really only mental structures. They have material form only so long as they are observed as such. Strange as it may sound, this is now accepted truth.

We have discovered that the closer we examine energy, the more readily it disappears into consciousness. To be sure, the physical world continues to exist. But this existence should be viewed as an effect and not a cause of things—as a vessel of energy and not the energy itself.

Taking this concept one step further, energy is an expression of thought and intelligence. Unfortunately, we are not prepared to deal with our physical world in terms of intelligence or thought. It is too great a step at this moment in time to jump from a physical perception of our universe to one which is metaphysical. Seeing objects around us as "energy" or "intelligence" will require an enormous adjustment.

Spiritual people or those with unusual psychic abilities are attuned to this consciousness. Through spiritual activity demonstrated by their Desire to Share, they have removed the obstructions that encumber others. Moreover, these people are often able to bring elevated states of awareness to others.

The nature of energy and intelligence as expressions of a single force will likely confuse many readers. However, there is a growing tendency among researchers to agree that the mind and the brain are not the same. Intelligence as such cannot be found within the framework of the organic brain. The enormous network of neurons and nerve responses in the brain can now be mapped, detected, and meticulously followed by scientists. Yet intelligence and consciousness itself continue to elude them. The cells, molecules, sub-atomic particles, and other physical segments have very little to say as to what is really going on in the brain. These external entities seem merely to transfer or make manifest intelligence. Similarly, energy fields serve as channels through which internal intelligence forces find their expression.

The inner intelligence within one's own magnetic field also flows out of the individual's body, forming a sphere of activity that may extend as far as seven feet. This phenomenon is the aura—an image of the energy- intelligences of one's life processes. Auras essentially represent transcendence of the material dimension. And even though they are bound up with and connected to the structure and content of the body, they have their own metaphysical laws and principles concerning time, space, and motion.

From the kabbalistic perspective, auras have been known to extend themselves beyond the usual limitation of several feet. In fact, if you're still not certain as to what I have been alluding to, let me state it as clearly as I can: teleportation.

Teleportation is the theoretical transportation of matter through space that is accomplished by converting matter into energy and then reconverting it at a terminal point. Can one actually be transported through space? Can we really appear to others at other ends of the earth?

Consider this: In dreams, we apparently travel through space. We can, for example, go forward or backward in time. In our dreams, we may also make contact with people or relatives who have since passed on. And while this out-of-body experience is not quite identical to teleportation, a separation from the ordinary limits of the physical world has nonetheless been brought about; we do experience ourselves as separate from our physical body. Indeed, such nightly out-of-body experiences are now being explored in scientific investigations.

Regarding the phenomenon of teleportation, most of us have already had this experience. How many times have friends remarked to us that they could have sworn they had seen us at a place they had visited? We are certain that they must have mistaken us for someone else; undoubtedly, we respond, the person they saw was someone who probably just looked like us. In some cases our friends are particularly emphatic, but to their dismay, they are told it really wasn't us. Was this an illusion, or can one really be in two places at the same time?

Kabbalah considers the possibility of energy-intelligence transfer as something very real, citing several examples
in which the energy-intelligence of one individual became
manifested elsewhere. For example, *The Zohar* describes the
purchase of a place for burial by Abraham for his wife Sarah:

So the field of Ephron, which was in Machpelah, which
was before Mamre, the field, and the cave which was therein,
and all the trees that were in the field, that were in all the bor-
ders round about, were made unto Abraham for a possession.

Rav Judah discoursed on this verse and said:

> Abraham recognized the cave of
> Machpelah by a certain sign, and he had long set
> his mind and heart on it. For he had once
> entered that cave and seen Adam and Eve con-
> cealed there. How did he recognize Adam and
> Eve inasmuch as he never met them before?
> [They had died long before.] Answered Rav
> Judah: He knew that they were Adam and Eve
> because he saw the form of Adam very clearly,
> and while he was gazing at the form, a door
> opened into the Garden of Eden. He perceived
> the same form standing there also near the door.
> Now, Abraham knew that whoever looks at the
> form of Adam cannot escape death. For when a
> person is about to pass out of this world he
> catches sight of Adam, and at that moment he
> dies. Abraham, however, did look at him, saw his
> form and yet survived. He saw, moreover, a shin-
> ing light that lit up the cave, and a lamp burning.

Abraham then coveted that cave for his burial place, and his mind and heart were set upon it.

If we choose to accept these words of *The Zohar*—if we admit that we have all undergone an experience with a person no longer among the living—an understanding of teleportation will come easily. *The Zohar* goes to great lengths to remove any doubts as to what Abraham really saw. From a Zoharic standpoint, Abraham did not hallucinate. He definitely saw Adam.

Teleportation might be compared to a live television program—one in which the participants are transferred into the home of the viewer without regard to distance. Some years later, although the participants may have died, their forms continue to be projected over television waves.

Men of science are well aware that we have not discovered the limits of form transmission, as indicated in *The Zohar*. Therefore, I feel that such a theory, if applied, will survive the many serious research and investigative projects that this book shall initiate.

It would seem to be stretching the laws of teleportation a bit if we are asked to consider a conversation between the living and the energy- intelligence of one who is deceased. Yet this very phenomenon is described in the following Zohar passage:

And the field and the cave that is therein arose—that is, there was literally an arising before the presence of Abraham. Up until that time nothing had been visible, but now what

had been hidden rose up and became visible.
Rav Shimon said: "When Abraham brought
Sarah in there for burial, Adam and Eve arose
and refused to receive her." They said: "Is not
our shame already great enough before the Lord
in the other world on account of our sin, which
brought death into the world, that you should
come to shame us further with your good
deeds?" Abraham answered: "I am already destined to make atonement before the Lord for
you, so you may nevermore be ashamed before
Him." Forthwith Abraham after this buried
Sarah his wife to wit after Abraham had taken
upon himself this obligation. Adam then
returned to his place, but not Eve, until
Abraham came and placed her beside Adam who
received her for Abraham's sake.

Clearly, in the tale of Machpelah and a good many
other cases detailed in *The Zohar*, there is more at work than
extrasensory perception, spirit possession, reincarnation, and
hallucinations. Can the reader of this book concede that teleportation might well be that "something more"?

Kabbalah abounds with intriguing tales of teleportation and the vast knowledge necessary for its implementa-
tion. Unfortunately, grave abuses have been committed in
the name of spirituality. Recently, for example, there has
been a growing interest in paranormal powers, altered states
of consciousness, and similar phenomena. Although these
pursuits have for the most part been legitimate, many indi-

viduals have innocently become involved with less desirable movements in their quest to reach their goals. And in the process, they have been misled.

Down through the ages, a number of highly advanced spiritual teachers have emerged, including the Ari, Rav Ashlag, and Rav Brandwein. The majority of their students received only a limited degree of wisdom acceptable to their level of spiritual awareness. Students would have to demonstrate their degree of sharing and understanding of the concept "love thy neighbor." This would be an indication as to whether they had the ability to correctly make use of the information before it was made available to them. The followers of these masters would be given certain teachings as they were preparing themselves to use this wisdom wisely. The sinking of the continent Atlantis, discussed earlier, served to illustrate how this wisdom—and the misuse thereof—resulted in the eventual destruction and disappearance of an advanced civilization.

The question likely to be raised at this time is, "Are we to accept *The Zohar*, the writings of the Ari, and those of other known kabbalists as accurate?" There cannot be one answer for all. The mystical expression "When the student is ready, the master will appear" holds for all who seek truth. For all who are ready to accept Kabbalah, Kabbalah reveals itself.

By virtue of the fact that you have reached the last page of *Wheels of a Soul*, I am certain that you are among that number. And I am equally certain that all humanity will soon be by your side.

If you were inspired by this book in any way and would like to know how you can continue to enrich your life through the wisdom of Kabbalah, here is what you can do next:

Call 1-800-KABBALAH where trained instructors are available 18 hours a day. These dedicated people are willing to answer any and all questions about Kabbalah and help guide you along in your effort to learn more.

More Books that can bring the wisdom of Kabbalah into your life

God Wears Lipstick
By Karen Berg

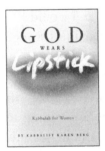

God Wears Lipstick is written exclusively for women (or for men who better want to understand women) by one of the driving forces behind the Kabbalah movement.

For thousands of years, women were banned from studying Kabbalah, the ancient source of wisdom that explains who we are and what our purpose is in this universe.

Karen Berg changed that. She opened the doors of The Kabbalah Centre to anyone who wanted to understand the wisdom of Kabbalah and brought Light to these people.

In *God Wears Lipstick*, Karen Berg shares that wisdom with us, especially as it affects you and your relationships. She reveals a woman's special place in the universe and why women have a spiritual advantage over men. She explains how to find your soulmate and your purpose in life. She empowers you to become a better human being as you connect to the Light, and she then gives you the tools for living and loving.

The Power of You
By Rav Berg

For the past 5,000 years, neither science nor psychology has been able to solve the fundamental problem of chaos in people's lives.

Now, one man is providing the answer. He is Kabbalist Rav Berg.

Beneath the pain and chaos that disrupts our lives, Kabbalist Rav Berg brings to light a hidden realm of order, purpose, and unity. Revealed is a universe in which mind becomes master over matter—a world in which God, human thought, and the entire cosmos are mysteriously interconnected.

Join this generation's premier Kabbalist on a mind-bending journey along the cutting edge of reality. Peer into the vast reservoir of spiritual wisdom that is Kabbalah, where the secrets of creation, life, and death have remained hidden for thousands of years.

The Red String: The Power of Protection
By Yehuda Berg

Read the book that everyone is wearing!

Discover the ancient technology that empowers and fuels the hugely popular Red String, the most widely recognized tool of Kabbalistic wisdom. Yehuda Berg, author of the international best-seller *The 72 Names of God: Technology for the Soul*, continues to reveal the secrets of the world's oldest and most powerful wisdom with his new book, *The Red String: The Power of Protection*. Discover the antidote to the negative effects of the dreaded "Evil Eye" in this second book of the Technology for the Soul series.

Find out the real power behind the Red String and why millions of people won't leave home without it.

It's all here. Everything you wanted to know about the Red String but were afraid to ask!

The Dreams: Finding Your Way in the Dark
By Yehuda Berg

In *The Dreams Book*, the debut installment of the Technology for the Soul Series, national best-selling author Yehuda Berg lifts the curtain of reality to reveal secrets of dream interpretation that have remained hidden for centuries.

Readers will discover a millennia-old system for understanding dreams and will learn powerful techniques to help them find soul mates, discover career opportunities, be alerted to potential illness in the body, improve relationships with others, develop an overall deeper awareness, and much more.

The dream state is a mysterious and fascinating realm in which the rules of reality do not apply. This book is the key to navigating the dreamscape, where the answers to all of life's questions await.

Becoming Like God
By Michael Berg

At the age of 16, kabbalistic scholar Michael Berg began the herculean task of translating *The Zohar*, Kabbalah's chief text, from its original Aramaic into its first complete English translation. *The Zohar*, which consists of 23 volumes, is considered a compendium of virtually all information pertaining to the universe, and its wisdom is only beginning to be verified today.

During the ten years he worked on *The Zohar*, Michael Berg discovered the long-lost secret for which humanity has searched for more than 5,000 years: how to achieve our ultimate destiny. *Becoming Like God* reveals the transformative method by which people can actually break free of what is called "ego nature" to achieve total joy and lasting life.

Berg puts forth the revolutionary idea that for the first time in history, an opportunity is being made available to humankind: an opportunity to Become Like God.

The Secret
By Michael Berg

Like a jewel that has been painstakingly cut and polished, *The Secret* reveals life's essence in its most concise and powerful form. Michael Berg begins by showing you how our everyday understanding of our purpose in the world is literally backwards. Whenever there is pain in our lives—indeed, whenever there is anything less than complete joy and fulfillment—this basic misunderstanding is the reason.

The Kabbalah Centre

The International Leader in the Education of Kabbalah

Since its founding, The Kabbalah Centre has had a single mission: to improve and transform people's lives by bringing the power and wisdom of Kabbalah to all who wish to partake of it.

Through the lifelong efforts of Rav Berg, his wife Karen, and the great spiritual lineage of which they are a part, an astonishing 3.5 million people around the world have already been touched by the powerful teachings of Kabbalah. And each year, the numbers are growing!

As the leading source of Kabbalistic wisdom with 50 locations around the world, The Kabbalah Centre offers you a wealth of resources, including:

- The English Zohar, the first-ever comprehensive English translation of the foundation of Kabbalistic wisdom. In 23 beautifully bound volumes, this edition includes the full Aramaic text, the English translation, and detailed commentary, making this once-inaccessible text understandable to all.

- A full schedule of workshops, lectures, and evening classes for students at all levels of knowledge and experience.

- CDs, audiotapes and videotapes, and books in English and ten other languages.

- One of the Internet's most exciting and comprehensive websites, **www.kabbalah.com**—which receives more than 100,000 visitors each month.

- A constantly expanding list of events and publications to help you live the teachings of Kabbalah with greater understanding and excitement.

Discover why The Kabbalah Centre is one of the world's fastest-growing spiritual organizations. Our sole purpose is to improve people's lives through the teachings of Kabbalah. Let us show you what Kabbalah can do for you!

Each Kabbalah Centre location hosts free introductory lectures. For more information on Kabbalah or on these and other products and services, call 1-800-KABBALAH.

Wherever you are, there's a Kabbalah Centre—because now you can call 1-800-KABBALAH from almost anywhere, 18 hours a day, and get answers or guidance right over the telephone. You'll be connected to distinguished senior faculty who are on hand to help you understand Kabbalah as deeply as you want to—whether it involves recommending a course of study; deciding which books/tapes to take or the order in which to take them; discussing the material; or anything else you wish to know about Kabbalah.

THE ZOHAR

"Bringing The Zohar from near oblivion to wide accessibility has taken many decades. It is an achievement of which we are truly proud and grateful."

—Michael Berg

Composed more than 2,000 years ago, *The Zohar* is a set of 23 books, a commentary on biblical and spiritual matters in the form of conversations among spiritual masters. But to describe *The Zohar* only in physical terms is greatly misleading. In truth, *The Zohar* is nothing less than a powerful tool for achieving the most important purposes of our lives. It was given to all humankind by the Creator to bring us protection, to connect us with the Creator's Light, and ultimately to fulfill our birthright of true spiritual transformation.

Eighty years ago, when The Kabbalah Centre was founded, *The Zohar* had virtually disappeared from the world. Few people in the general population had ever heard of it. Whoever sought to read it—in any country, in any language, at any price—faced a long and futile search.

Today all this has changed. Through the work of The Kabbalah Centre and the editorial efforts of Michael Berg, *The Zohar* is now being brought to the world, not only in the original Aramaic language but also in English.

The new English Zohar provides everything for connecting to this sacred text on all levels: the original Aramaic text for scanning; an English translation; and clear, concise commentary for study and learning.

May the words within this book

Open your heart and soul to the Light of Kabbalah

Spread its wisdom and truth throughout the world

Elevate the soul of my father, David ben Aaron Minoff

Bring success and blessings to my daughter Beth

And reunite me with the other half of my soul.